Quality Software Series: Volume 2

WHY SOFTWARE GETS IN TROUBLE

by

Gerald M. Weinberg

* * * * *

PUBLISHED BY:

Weinberg & Weinberg

Quality Software Series, Volume 2

Why Software Gets In Trouble

Copyright © 2014 by Gerald M. Weinberg

Table of Contents

New Preface

"Teachers not only teach, but they also learn." - Sauk saying

This book is the second half of a kind of an Anniversary present, commemorating my now-50-year love affair with computers. In the 40 years since I first sat at my computer to write down what I had learned in my first 40 years in the computer business, I've learned an enormous amount. Much of it has been written in the second, third, and fourth volumes of *Software Quality Management*. Some has been written in a variety of other books and articles, including, *Amplifying Your Effectiveness* (edited with Naomi Karten and James Bach), *What Did You Say? : The Art of Giving and Receiving Feedback* (with Edie and Charlie Seashore; *Perfect Software--and Other Illusions About Testing*; the *Roundtable on Project Management* and the *Roundtable on Technical Leadership* (both edited with Jim Bullock, and Marie Benesh); *Weinberg on Writing: The Fieldstone Method*; and *More Secrets of Consulting: The Consultant's Self-Esteem Tool Kit*.

There are also my novels, including, so far, the *Aremac* series, the *Stringers* series, *Earth's Endless Effort*, *Mistress of Molecules*, *Freshman Murders*, and *The Hands of God*–each of which attempts

1

to bring lessons to the reader through the medium of compelling stories of adventure. And one of the major reasons I've been writing novels and in other formats is what I've learned from reader feedback.

Typical of this learning when I read a book review written by my good friend, Dan Starr. About somebody else's book, he wrote, "This book is a gold mine." The next time I saw him, I asked him why he never called one of *my* books a gold mine.

"You know what a gold mine is like," he replied. "There are a few gold nuggets, but you have to sift through tons of worthless tailings to find them."

I was starting to feel better, but then he added, "Your books are more like coal mines."

"Oh?" was all I could muster.

"Yes. You know what a coal mine is like. Every shovelful contains something worthwhile. Every one."

I'm satisfied to be writing coal mines. Oh, sure, I once imagined that I could write a book in which every sentence, every word, would be 24-karat gold, but *nobody* can sustain that level for an entire book. Even the "Greatest Book Ever Written" has long boring, repetitious passages that not even the most ardent evangelist will ever quote. So, if even God won't write a solid gold book, I'm content to drop that particular fantasy.

But, readers tell me that compared with lots of other books, my books are dense, dense, reading. A common complaint about the Quality Software Management Series is this: "They're just too expensive and too big to take in all at once." So, when Volume I went out of print for a while (they're also expensive to print), I took another look and decided to break it into smaller, less expensive volumes.

The contents of first volume, *How Software Is Built*, are quite adequately explained by its title. So are the contents of this volume, *Why Software Gets In Trouble*. Another one of my books, *Perfect Software and Other Illusions about Testing*, makes an appropriate sequel to this one. After that comes Volumes 2, 3, and 4 of *Quality Software Management*, which I think will require further splitting for my audience today. In any case, each can be read on its own, or as part of the series.

I also learned that for many potential readers outside of the United States, simply paying the shipping for one of those volumes more than doubled the cost—in American dollars, no less. So, to make them available to non-Americans (and some Americans, too), I've chosen to make eBook versions, as well.

I've also learned that much of the "heaviness" of those volumes came from all the scholarly material, such as footnotes and references. Nowadays, with search engines on the internet, readers who wish to follow up on something they read don't really need those references. By omitting them, I make the volumes lighter, and shorter. And friendlier to the average modern reader.

The principal contents, on the other hand, are largely unchanged. I was writing about general principles–illustrated by specific examples–much of which derived from my *Introduction to General Systems Thinking* and *General Principles of System Design* (with Dani Weinberg). There are, of course, new examples from the Internet Age, but the fundamental principles remain the same.

For the modern reader, I suggest they add *Practice* problems based on their more recent experiences. For me to add such examples throughout would be such an overwhelming task it would delay the books by a number of years. And that's one more thing I hear from my readers: " "Get the books out there for us. Don't delay!"

One more explanation. I've taken the word "management" out of the sub-title, leaving, simply, *Quality Software*. Why? Because too many people who should be reading this material interpreted "management" to mean "managers." Certainly these books are for managers, but they're also for everyone else in the business of producing quality software.

I've learned anew that most of the improvements in our business do not come from managers, but from underneath. As many have said, "Change always comes from the bottom. Nobody holding four Aces has ever asked for a new deal." And that's why I'm hoping that these format changes will empower everybody to create a new deal in software.

Part IV. Fault Patterns

Three of the great discoveries of our time have to do with programming: the programming of computers, the programming of inheritance through DNA, and the programming of the human mind (psychoanalysis). In each case, the idea of *error* plays a central role.

The first of these discoveries was psychoanalysis, with which Sigmund Freud opened the Twentieth Century and set a tone for the other two. In his introductory lectures, Freud opened the human mind to inspection through the use of errors—what we now call "Freudian slips."

The second of these discoveries was DNA. Once again, key clues to the workings of inheritance were offered by the study of errors, such as mutations, which were mistakes in transcribing the genetic code from one generation to the next.

The third of these discoveries was the stored program computer. From the first, the pioneers considered error a central concern. von Neumann noted that the largest part of natural organisms was devoted to the problem of survival in the face of error, and that the programmer of a computer need be similarly concerned.

In all three of these great discoveries, errors were treated not as lapses in intelligence, or moral failures, or insignificant trivialities—all common attitudes in the past. Instead, errors were treated as *sources of valuable information*, on which great discoveries could be based.

The treatment of error as a source of valuable information is precisely what distinguishes the feedback (error-controlled) system from its less capable predecessors—and thus distinguishes Steering software cultures from Patterns 1 and 2. Organizations in those patterns have more traditional—and less productive—attitudes about the role of errors in software development, attitudes that they will have to change if they are to transform themselves into Pattern 3 organizations.

So, in the following chapters, we'll explore what happens to Pattern 1 and especially Pattern 2 organizations as they battle those "inevitable" errors in their software. After reading these chapters, perhaps they'll appreciate that they can never move to a Steering pattern until they learn how to use the information in the errors they make.

Chapter 1: Observing and Reasoning About Errors

Men are not moved by things, but by the views which they take of them.- Epictetus

One of my editors complained that the first sections of this chapter spend "an inordinate amount of time on semantics, relative to the thorny issues of software failures and their detection." What I wanted to say to her, and what I will say to you, is that "semantics" are one of the roots of "the thorny issues of software failures and their detection." Therefore, I need to start this part of the book by clearing up some of the most subversive ideas and definitions about failure. If you already have a perfect understanding of software failure, then skim quickly, and please forgive me.

1.1. Conceptual Errors About Errors

1.1.1. Errors are not a moral issue

"What do you do with a person who is 900 pounds overweight that approaches the problem without even wondering how a person gets to be 900 pounds overweight?" - Tom DeMarco

This is the question Tom DeMarco asked when he read an early version of the upcoming chapters. He was exasperated about clients who were having trouble managing more than 10,000 error reports per product. So was I.

Over thirty years ago, in my first book on computer programming, Herb Leeds and I emphasized what we then considered the first principle of programming:

The best way to deal with errors is not to make them in the first place.

In those days, like many hotshot programmers, I meant "best" in a *moral* sense:

(1) Those of us who don't make errors are better than those of you who do.

I still consider this the first principle of programming, but somehow I no longer apply any *moral* sense to the principle, but only an *economic* sense:

(2) Most errors cost more to handle than they cost to prevent.

This, I believe, is part of what Crosby means when he says "quality is free." But even if it were a moral question, in sense (1), I don't think that Pattern 3 cultures—which do a great deal to prevent errors—can claim any moral superiority over Pattern 1 and Pattern 2 cultures—which do not. You cannot say that someone is morally inferior because they don't do something they *cannot* do, and Pattern 1 and Pattern 2 software cultures, where most programmers reside, are *culturally incapable* of preventing large numbers of errors. Why? Let me put Tom's question another way:

"What do you do with a person who is rich, admired by thousands, overloaded with exciting work, 900 pounds overweight, and has 'no problem' except for occasional work lost because of back problems?"

Tom's question *presumes* that the thousand pound person perceives a *weight* problem, but what if they perceive a *back* problem. My Pattern 1 and 2 clients with tens of thousands of errors in their software do not perceive they have a serious problem with errors. They are making money, and they are winning the praise of their customers. On two products out of three, the complaints are generally at a tolerable level. With their rate of profit, who cares if a third of their projects have to be written off as a total loss?

If I attempt to discuss these mountains of errors with Pattern 1 and 2 clients, they reply, "In programming, errors are inevitable, but we've got them more or less under control. Don't worry about *errors*. We want you to help us get things out on *schedule*." They see no more connection between enormous error rates and two-year schedule slippages than the obese person sees between 900 pounds of body fat and pains in the back. Can I accuse them of having the wrong moral attitude about errors? I might just as well accuse a blind person of having the wrong moral attitude about the rainbow.

But it is a moral question for me, their consultant. If my thousand-pound client is *happy*, it's not my business to tell him how to lose weight. If he comes to me with back problems, I can show him through a diagram of effects how weight affects his back. Then it's up to *him* to decide how much pain is worth how many chocolate cakes.

1.1.2. Quality is not the same thing as absence of errors

Errors in software used to be a moral issue for me, and still are for many writers. Perhaps that's why these writers have asserted that "quality is the absence of errors." It must be a moral issue for them, because otherwise it would be a grave error in reasoning. Here's how their reasoning might have gone wrong. Perhaps they observed that when their work is interrupted by numerous software errors, they can't appreciate any other good software qualities. From this observation, they can conclude that many errors will make software worthless—i.e., zero quality.

But here's the fallacy: *Though copious errors guarantee worthlessness, but zero errors guarantees nothing at all about the value of software.*

Let's take one example. Would you offer me $100 for a zero defect program to compute the horoscope of Philip Amberly Warblemaxon, who died in 1927 after a 37-year career as a filing clerk in a hat factory in Akron? I doubt it, because to have value, software must be *more than perfect*. It must be *useful to someone*.

Still, I would never deny the importance of errors. First of all, if I did, Pattern 1 and Pattern 2 organizations would stop reading this book. To them, chasing errors is as natural as chasing sheep is to a German Shepherd Dog. And, as we've seen, when they see the rather different life of a Pattern 3 organization, they simply don't believe it.

Second of all, I do know that when errors run away from us, we have lost quality. Perhaps our customers will tolerate 10,000 errors, but, as Tom DeMarco asked me, will they tolerate 10,000,000,000,000,000,000,000,000,000? In this sense, errors *are* a matter of quality. Therefore, we must train people to make *fewer* errors, while at the same time managing the errors they do make, to keep them from running away.

1.1.3. The terminology of error

I've sometimes found it hard to talk about the dynamics of error in software because there are many different ways of talking about errors themselves. One of the best ways for a consultant to assess the software engineering maturity of an organization is by the language they use, particularly the language they use to discuss error. To take an obvious example, those who call everything "bugs" are a long way from taking responsibility for controlling their own process. Until they start using precise and accurate language, there's little sense in teaching such people about basic dynamics.

Faults and failures. First of all, it pays to distinguish between failures (the symptoms) and faults (the diseases). Musa gives these definitions:

A failure "is the departure of the external results of program operation from requirements."

A fault "is the defect in the program that, when executed under particular conditions, causes a failure."

For example:

An accounting program had a incorrect instruction (fault) in the formatting routine that inserts commas in large numbers such as "$4,500,000". Any time a user prints a number greater than six digits, a comma may be missing (a failure). Many failures resulted from this one fault.

How many failures result from a single fault? That depends on

• the location of the fault

• how long the fault remains before it is removed

• how many people are using the software.

The comma-insertion fault led to millions of failures because it was in a frequently used piece of code, in software that has thousands of users, and it remained unresolved for more than a year.

When studying error reports in various clients, I often find that they mix failures and faults in the same statistics, because they don't understand the distinction. If these two different measures are mixed into one, it will be difficult to understand their own experiences. For instance, because a single fault can lead to many failures, it would be impossible to compare failures between two organizations who aren't careful in making this "semantic" distinction.

Organization A has 100,000 customers who use their software product for an average of 3 hours a day. Organization B has a single customer who uses one software system once a month. Organization A produces 1 fault per thousand lines of code, and receives over 100 complaints a day. Organization B produces 100 faults per thousand lines of code, but receives only one complaint a month.

Organization A claims they are better software developers than Organization B. Organization B claims they are better software developers than Organization A. Perhaps they're both right.

The System Trouble Incident (STI). Because of the important distinction between faults and failures, I encourage my clients to keep at least two different statistics. The first of these is a data base of "system trouble incidents," or STIs. In this book, I'll mean an STI to be an "incident report of one failure as experienced by a customer or simulated customer (such as a tester)."

I know of no industry standard nomenclature for these reports —except that they invariably take the form of TLAs (Three Letter Acronyms). The TLAs I have encountered include:

• STR, for "software trouble report"

- SIR, for "software incident report," or "system incident report"
- SPR, for "software problem report," or "software problem record"
- MDR, for "malfunction detection report"
- CPI, for "customer problem incident"
- SEC, for "significant error case,"
- SIR, for "software issue report"
- DBR, for "detailed bug report," or "detailed bug record"
- SFD, for "system failure description"
- STD, for "software trouble description," or "software trouble detail"

I generally try to follow my client's naming conventions, but try hard to find out exactly what is meant. I encourage them to use unique, descriptive names. It tells me a lot about a software organization when they use more than one TLA for the same item. Workers in that organization are confused, just as my readers would be confused if I kept switching among ten TLAs for STIs. The reasons I prefer STI to some of the above are as follows:

1. It makes no prejudgment about the fault that led to the failure. For instance, it might have been a misreading of the manual, or a mistyping that wasn't noticed. Calling it a bug, an error, a failure, or a problem, tends to mislead.

2. Calling it a "trouble incident" implies that once upon a time, somebody, somewhere, was sufficiently troubled by something that they happened to bother making a report. Since our definition of quality is "value to some person," someone being troubled implies that it's *worth* something to look at the STI.

3. The words "software" and "code" also contain a presumption of *guilt*, which may unnecessarily restrict location and correction activities. We might correct an STI with a code fix, but we might also change a manual, upgrade a training program, change our ads or our sales pitch, furnish a help message, change the design, or let it stand unchanged. The word "system" says to me that any part of the overall system may contain the fault, and any part (or parts) may receive the corrective activity.

4. The word "customer" excludes troubled people who don't happen to be customers, such as programmers, analysts, salespeople, managers, hardware engineers, or testers. We should be so happy to receive reports of troublesome incidents *before* they get to customers that we wouldn't want to discourage anybody.

Similar principles of semantic precision might guide your own design of TLAs, to remove one more source of error, or one more impediment to their removal. Pattern 3 organizations always use TLAs more precisely than do Pattern 1 and 2 organizations.

System Fault Analysis(SFA). The second statistic is a database of information on faults, which I call SFA, for System

Fault Analysis. Few of my clients initially keep such a database separate from their STIs, so I haven't found such a diversity of TLAs. Ed Ely tells me, however, that he has seen the name RCA, for "Root Cause Analysis." Since RCA would never do, the name SFA is a helpful alternative because:

1. It clearly speaks about faults, not failures. This is an important distinction. No SFA is created until a fault has been identified. When a SFA is created, it is tied back to *as many STIs as possible*. The time lag between the earliest STI and the SFA that clears it up can be an important dynamic measure.

2. It clearly speaks about the system, so the database can contain fault reports for faults found anywhere in the system.

3. The word "analysis" correctly implies that data is the result of careful thought, and is not to be completed unless and until someone is quite sure of their reasoning.

"Fault" does not imply blame. One deficiency with the semantics of the term"fault" is the possible implication of *blame*, as opposed to *information*. In an SFA, we must be careful to distinguish two places associated with a fault, either of these implies anything about whose "fault" it was:

a. *origin*: at what stage in our process the fault originated

b. *correction*: what part(s) of the system will be changed to remedy the fault

Pattern 1 and 2 organizations tend to equate these two

notions, but the motto, "you broke it, you fix it," often leads to an unproductive "blame game." "Correction" tells us where it was wisest, under the circumstances, to make the changes, regardless of what put the fault there in the first place. For example, we might decide to change the documentation—not because the documentation was bad, but because the design is so poor it needs more documenting and the code is so tangled we don't dare try to fix it there.

If Pattern 3 organizations are not heavily into blaming, why would they want to record "origin" of a fault? To these organizations, "Origin" merely suggests where action might be taken to *prevent* a similar fault in the future, not which employee is to be taken out and crucified. Analyzing origins, however, requires skill and experience to determine the earliest possible prevention moment in our process. For instance, an error in the code might have been prevented if the requirements document were more clearly written. In that case, we should say that the "origin" was in the requirements stage.

1.2. Mis-classification of Error-Handling Processes

By the term "error-handling process," we'll refer to the overall pattern that has to do with errors, a pattern which can be resolved into several activities. Once we understand the distinction among these component activities, we'll be able to describe the dynamics of each in a way that will suggest improvement. Characteristically, however, Pattern 1 and Pattern 2 organizations are not very adept at knowing just precisely what their error-handling process is. If you ask, the typical answer will be "debugging." With that sort of imprecise speech, improvement in fault-handling is unlikely.

1.2.1. Detection

Detection of faults is achieved in different ways in different software cultures. Pattern 1 and 2 organizations tend to depend on faults being detected by *failures* in some sort of machine execution of code, such as machine software testing, beta testing, and operational use by customers. These are the STIs.

Pattern 3 organizations also detect faults though failures, but tend to prefer going *directly to faults* by some process that does not require machine execution of the code. These mechanisms include accident (such as running into an error while looking in code for something else), technical reviews of great variety, and tools that process code, designs, and requirements as analyzable documents, suggesting failures without machine execution of the code itself. These methods result in SFA which don't necessarily correspond to any STI, if they were applied early enough to prevent any failure resulting from the fault.

1.2.2. Location

Location, or isolation, is the process of matching failures with faults. Even when a fault is found directly, as in a code review, good practice dictates that the SFA contain a trace forward into the set of failures known to exist. Only by forward tracing can unsolved failures be cleared out of the STI data base. If a great many unsolved STIs remain, managers and programmers have a tendency to discount all of them, which makes location of truly active STIs more difficult.

1.2.3. Resolution

Resolution is the process that ensures that a fault no longer exists, or that a failure will never occur again. A failure may be solved without having its fault or faults removed. Removal of faults is an optional process, but resolution is not. Resolution of an STI *may* be performed in several ways:

1. Remove the fault that led to the STI. This is the "classic" way of "debugging."

2. Define the STI as unimportant, such as "too minor to fix," or "non-reproducible."

3. Define the STI as not arising from a fault in the system, but usually as a fault in the person who reported it.

4. Define the fault as not a fault, such as by following the Bolden Rule that says, "If you can't fix it, feature it."

In troubled Pattern 2 organizations, the majority of STIs are resolved by 2, 3, and 4, while management believes they are resolved by (1).

1.2.4. Prevention

Prevention may seem a pie-in-the sky approach to people buried deep in Pattern 1 and Pattern 2 organizations. The history of other engineering disciplines assures us that some schemes for preventing errors will ultimately prevail, but these seem a long way from where most of my clients are standing today. When I show them articles about Pattern 3 organizations, they say they're not applicable to their organizations. When I show them articles about "clean room" software development or other Pattern 4 techniques, they simply chuckle with disbelief.

In fact, however, most of the error work in a software development organization is actually prevention work, though Pattern 2 managers don't understand this. Only after they become rather sophisticated in analyzing software engineering dynamics do they realize that most of their activities are in place to *prevent* error, not fix it. Just to take one example, ask people why they follow the practice of "design before code." Very few of them will recognize this rule as an error-prevention strategy dictated by the war against the Size/Complexity Dynamic.

1.2.5. Distribution

In Pattern 2 organizations, *distribution* of errors is an important and often time-consuming activity. By distribution, we mean any activity that serves to prevent attributing errors to one part of the organization *by using the technique moving them to*

21

another place. Here are some examples of distribution:

1. Developers quickly throw code "over the wall" to testers, so that errors are seen as somehow arising during test, rather than from coding.

2. The organization skips the design reviews so that design faults are seen as coding faults.

3. Testers pass code into operations so problems can be classified as "maintenance faults."

These three examples are the type of distribution activity that prevents *blame*, in response to measurement systems that are used punitively rather than for control activities. When you don't know how to prevent errors, what else can you do but prevent blame for errors? Of course, to the extent that the workers are playing "hot potato" with faults, they have that much less time to do actual productive work. We'll see more about the hot potato phenomenon when we study the dynamics of management pressure.

But not all distribution activities are disguised forms of hot potato. Where blame is not the name of the game, distribution actually serves useful purposes. Pattern 3 organizations tend to distribute the faults *earlier* in the process than Pattern 2 organizations:

4. Design and requirements work are seen as ways of catching large scope faults early in the development process, rather

than later when they will be more costly to resolve.

5. User manuals are written early as a way of revealing faults in interface requirements and generating the basis for acceptance tests. Once again, this unburdens the late parts of the development cycle.

1.3. Observational Errors About Errors

Failure detection is a process of *noticing differences*— between what is desired and what exists. When we consider the cybernetic model of control, we understand how important seeing differences—failure detection—is to a feedback controller.

Giving things labels is a *substitute* for noticing. That's another reason I always emphasize the importance of the words controllers use. It's all too easy not to notice important differences if you name two things the same, or to see a difference where none exists if you name them differently.

1.3.1 Selection Fallacies

There is a whole class of common mislabelings which I call "selection fallacies." A selection fallacy occurs when a controller makes an incorrect linear assumption about observation that says, incorrectly,

> *"I don't have to observe the full set of data, because a more easily observed set of data adequately represents it."*

It's a fallacy because it doesn't take into account that the processes of selecting the two groups of data may be different, and thus conclusions drawn from one group may not apply to the other. Selection fallacies are easy to spot *after the fact*, but easy to fall into before, especially if we have some reason to *want* one conclusion more than another.

Completed vs. terminated projects. Here's an example of a common selection fallacy in software:

A client surveyed the number of faults produced per thousand lines of code (KLOC) in 152 projects. The study was done very carefully, using the SFA data base for each project. The study concluded that the average project produced 6-23 faults/KLOC, with an average of 14. They felt that this was in line with other organizations in their industry, so they had no strong motivation to invest in further reductions.

Listening to the presentation of this careful study, it would have been easy to miss the selection fallacy, but always being cautious, I asked, "How did you choose the 152 projects?"

"Oh, we were very careful not to bias the study," the presenter said. "We chose *every* project that was completed in a 3-month period."

"You emphasized the wrong word," I said, now seeing the selection fallacy.

"What do you mean?" he asked.

"You should have said, 'We chose every project that was *completed* in a 3-month period.' How many projects here are started that *never* complete?"

The presenter didn't know, and neither did anyone else in the room. I got them to give an approximation, which was later verified by a small study. Historically, in this organization, 27% of initiated projects were never completed. These projects accounted for over 40% of their development budget, because some were not abandoned for a long, long time. A sample of these projects showed a range of 19-145 faults/KLOC, with an average of 38. Later, when the average was weighted by project *size*, it grew to 86. The two biggest projects also had the highest faults/KLOC.

Where had they gone wrong? In presenting *completed* projects as representative of *all* projects, the presenters had committed a common selection fallacy which led the organization to believe that they were not too bad in their fault-producing performance. Then, when they presented *all failed projects* as typical of their *worst* projects, they committed the same fallacy in reverse. The second fallacy led them to miss the fact that they simply didn't know how to develop large projects, probably because they couldn't deal with the faults they generated.

Early vs. late users. Here's another common selection fallacy:

A software organization shipped an update to product X and tracked the STIs that arrived in the first two months. They used these to make a linear projection of the STI load they would have to handle in the following months. Their estimate of the number of STIs was quite accurate, but the total workload generated by those STIs was underestimated by a factor of 3.5.

They had committed several selection fallacies, all based on the assumption that early STIs would be typical of later STIs. They were not because,

1. Later STIs had a far higher failure/fault ratio, because more customers were using the system and encountering the same failures multiple times. The company had no efficient way of resolving these multiple reports of the same failure.

2. Early users of the update were not typical of late users. They tended to be more self-reliant, and worked around a number of failures that later users had to report as STIs in order to get help. Although they were easy to work around, their underlying faults were not necessarily easy to resolve.

3. Early users also tended to use a different set of features than the later users. The typical later user was later because their use was much more extensive, both in features covered and number of people having access to the system. These attributes meant that their installation procedure was more complex, thus slower, which is why they were later users. But more people accessing the system, using more of the features, meant many more STIs.

*"**He's just like me.**"* The selection fallacy works not only on the observations, but also on the *observers*. Here's the continuation of the story about Simon, the project manager who couldn't recognize tears.

After Simon asked me whether there was something in Herb's eye, I said, "Well, I really don't know. Why don't you ask him?"

"Oh, it's not really important enough to take the time," Simon replied. "I need to ask you how you think the project is going? I'm really pleased at what a great job Herb did, getting that program ready just a week late, after it was in so much trouble."

"Really?" I said. "I thought you were rather upset about the late delivery."

"Oh, that. Sure, I'd like to have had it on time, but it's no big deal."

"I think Herb thought it was a big deal."

"What makes you think that?"

"I believe he was upset when you yelled at him."

"Oh, no. Herb knows me too well to be upset, just because I raised my voice a little. He's just like me, so he knows I'm just an enthusiastic guy."

Simon committed a selection fallacy by assuming "he's just like me." The managers in a software organization are not "just like" the rest of the people—else why were they selected to be managers, and why are they being paid more money? Why not observe the other person instead of assuming the two of you are exactly alike?

Any manager who can't or won't see or hear other peoples' feelings is like a ship's captain trying to navigate at night without radar or sonar. Feelings are the radar and sonar of project life—reflections off the reefs and shoals and shallow bottoms on which your project can run aground. You can't do it with your eyes and ears closed, just using a map inside your own head, if only because you're not just like everyone else.

1.3.2. Getting observations backwards

It's one thing to fail to observe something correctly. It's quite another to observe correctly, but then to interpret the observations *backwards*, so that black is labeled white and white is labeled black. Some people have a hard time believing that a highly paid software engineering manager could actually label observations backwards, so here a few examples of hundreds I've observed.

Who are the best and the worst programmers?

A software development manager told me that he had a way to measure who were his best programmers and who were his worst. I was fascinated, so I asked him how he did it. He told me that he sat in his office and observed who was always out asking questions of users and other programmers. I thought this was a terrific measure, and I discussed it with him with great excitement. After a few minutes, however, I realized that he thought the programmers who spend the most time asking questions are his worst ones. I, on the other hand, thought that some of these were probably the best programmers in his shop.

Which is the good quality release?

When she received her first monthly STI summary for a newly released product, the vice-president of software technology waved it at me and said, "Well, we've finally put out a high-quality release." As it turned out, the release offered so little new function that essentially nobody bothered to install it. Hence, there were virtually no troubles reported. Later, when people did have to install it, they found that it was just as full of errors as all the previous releases.

Why is someone working late?

A programming team manager told me, "Josh is my best programmer. The reason he starts work in the afternoon and stays late at night is so he won't be disturbed by the less experienced programmers." It turned out that Josh was so ashamed of the poor quality of his work that he didn't want anyone to see how much trouble he was having.

Who knows what's right and wrong?

Another team leader told me, "Cynthia is angry because I showed her what was wrong with her program, and how it should have been done in the first place. I suppose you're going to tell me I have to learn to be more tactful." Cynthia showed me the program and what the team leader had said was wrong. It wasn't wrong at all. Cynthia said, "What ticks me off is working under a boss who's not only technically illiterate, but doesn't know how to listen. He approaches every problem with an open mouth."

Which process is eliminating problems?

A project manager told me, "We've abandoned technical reviews in this project. They were valuable at first, and we found a lot of problems. Now, however, they don't find much trouble—not enough to justify the expense." As it turned out, the reason there were no problems was that the programmers were conducting secret reviews, to hide their errors from the manager, who berated anyone whose product showed errors in the review. They had not abandoned technical reviews; they had abandoned the practice of telling their manager about their technical reviews.

Feedback controllers use observations of behavior to decide upon actions to eliminate undesired behaviors. They feed these actions back into the system and thus create a negative feedback loop to stabilize the system, as shown in Figure 1-1.

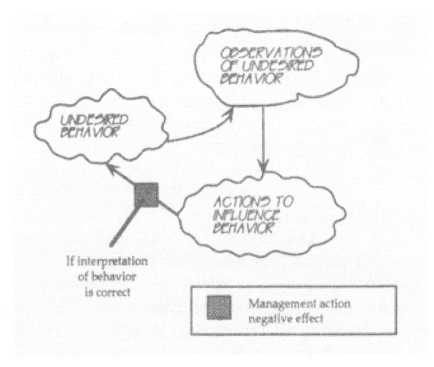

Figure 1-1. The feedback controller uses observations to decide upon actions to stabilize the system's behavior.

When the feedback controllers gets the meaning of the observation backwards, however, the designed actions create a positive feedback loop, actually encouraging the undesired behavior, as shown in Figure 1-2.

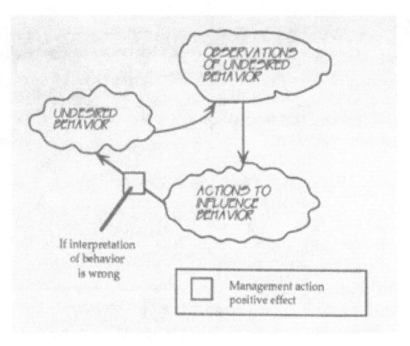

Figure 1-2. Getting the meaning of an observation backward creates an intervention loop that promotes what it should discourage and vice versa.

1.3.3. The Controller Fallacy

The example of eliminating technical reviews illustrates another common observational fallacy. Even if it were true that reviews were no longer finding errors, would that be the reason to abandon them? Technical reviews serve many functions in a software project, but one of their principal functions is to provide feedback information to be used in controlling the project. In other words, they are part of the controller's system.

It is the nature of feedback controllers to have an inverse

32

relationship to the systems they attempt to regulate.

• We spend money on a thermostat so we won't spend extra money on fuel for heating and cooling.

• We keep the fire department active so that fires will be inactive.

• We put constraints of the powers of government so that government won't put unnecessary constraints on the governed.

One result of this inverse relationship is this

The controller of a well-regulated system may not seem to be working hard.

But managers who don't understand this relationship often see lack of obvious controller activity as a sign that something is wrong with the control process. This is the Controller Fallacy, which comes in two forms:

If the controller isn't busy, it's not doing a good job.

If the controller is very busy, it must be a good controller.

Managers who believe the second form are the ones who "prove" how important they are by being too busy to see their workers.

The first form applies to the reversed technical review observation. If the technical reviews are not detecting a lot of mistakes, it could mean that the review system is broken. On the other hand, it could also mean that the review system is working very well, and preventing faults by such actions as

- motivating people to work with more precision

- raising awareness of the importance of quality work

- teaching people how to find faults before coming to reviews

- detecting indicators of poor work, before that work actually produces faults

- teaching people to prevent faults by using good techniques they see in reviews

1.4. Helpful Hints and Suggestions

- Usually, there are more failures than faults, but sometimes, there are faults that produce no failures—at least given the usage of the software up until the present time. And sometimes it takes more than one fault to equal one failure. For instance, there may be two that are "half-faults," neither of which would cause trouble except when used in conjunction with the other. In other cases, such as in performance errors, it may take an accumulation of small faults to equal a single failure. This makes it important to distinguish between functional failures and performance failures.

- Proliferation of acronyms is a sign of an organization's movement towards Pattern 2, where name magic is so important that a new name confers power on its creator. Care in designing acronyms is a sign of an organization's movement towards Pattern 3, where communication is so important.

34

• You can almost count on the fact that first customers aren't like later ones. Managers often commit a selection fallacy in planning their future as software vendors based on initial favorable customer reactions to a software system. The first customers are first because they are the ones the requirements fit for. Thus, they are very likely to be "like" the original designer/developers. Developers and customers communicate well, and think alike. This is not so as the number of customers grows, and explicit processes must be developed to replace this lost "natural" rapport.

• Selection fallacies are everywhere. You can protect yourself by wearing garlic flowers around your neck, or else by asking, whenever someone presents you with statistics to prove something, "Which cases are in your sample? Which cases are left out? What was the process by which you chose the cases you chose?

1.5 Summary

1. One of the reasons organizations have trouble dealing with software errors is the many conceptual errors they make concerning errors.

2. Some people make errors into a moral issue, losing track of the business justification for the way in which they are handled.

3. Quality is not the same thing as absence of errors, but the presence of many errors can destroy any other measures of quality in a product.

4. Organizations that don't handle error very well also don't talk very clearly about error. For instance, they frequently fail to distinguish faults from failures, or use faults to blame people in the organization.

5. Well functioning organizations can be recognized by the organized way they use faults and failures as information to control their process. The System Trouble Incident (STI) and the System Fault Analysis(SFA) are the fundamental sources of information about failures and faults.

6. Error-handling processes come in at least five varieties: detection, location, resolution, prevention, and distribution.

7. In addition to conceptual errors, there are a number of common observational errors people make about errors, including Selection Fallacies, getting observations backwards, and the Controller Fallacy

1.6. Practice

1. Here are some words I've heard used as synonyms for "fault" in software: lapse, slip, aberration, variation, minor variation, mistake, oversight, miscalculation, blooper, blunder, boner, miscue, fumble, botch, misconception, bug, error, failure. Add any words you've heard to the list, then put the list in order according to how much responsibility they imply on the human beings who created the fault.

2. When an organization begins the systematic practice of matching every failure with a known fault, it discovers that some failures have no corresponding fault. In Pattern 3 organizations, these failures are attributed to "process faults"—something wrong with their software process that either generated fictitious failures or prevents the isolation of real ones. List some examples of process faults commonly experienced in your own organization, such as careless filling out of STI records.

3. For a week, gather data about your organization in the following way: as you meet people in the normal course of events, ask them what they're doing. If it has anything to do with errors of any kind, make a note of how they label their activity—debugging, failure location, talking to a customer, or whatever. At the end of the week, summarize your findings in a report on the process categories used for error work in your organization's culture.

4. Describe a selection fallacy that you've experienced. Describe its consequences. How could a more appropriate selection have been made?

Chapter 2: The Failure Detection Curve

"We're ninety-nine percent complete!" (attributed to thousands of software project managers)

Throughout the history of the software business, people have been frustrated by the ever receding end of project after the project reaches "ninety-nine percent complete." In Pattern 2 organizations, the receding end is blamed on anyone who will stand still long enough to become a target. Pattern 3 organizations, on the other hand, know that underlying the "ninety-nine percent complete" is another dynamic, the Difference Detection Dynamic.

2.1 The Difference Detection Dynamic

Selection fallacies can have enormous consequences. A fascinating story of a world-wide selection fallacy is contained in an article by Root and Drew on "The Pattern of Petroleum Discovery Rates."

For many years, analysts had seriously overestimated oil recovery from regions, based on early drilling success. They had hypothesized all sorts of explanations for the failure of their models, but Root and Drew finally demonstrated that the failure of the models could be explained by a selection fallacy:

"First, most of the oil and gas discovered in a region is contained in a few large fields; and second, most of the large fields are discovered early in the exploration of the region."

Obviously, if you drill holes at random, you're more likely to hit somewhere in one of the big fields than one of the small ones. With trillions of dollars at stake, why did it take so long to discover this selection tautology? Are petroleum engineers stupid? Before we laugh at the petroleum engineers, we might save a chuckle for ourselves, the software engineers.

2.1.1 The Root-Drew fallacy in difference detection

The Root-Drew fallacy is committed every day in software development in trying to predict how long testing will take, based on early returns from testing. To understand how this happens, it will be useful to start by taking the little psychological test shown in Figure 2-1.

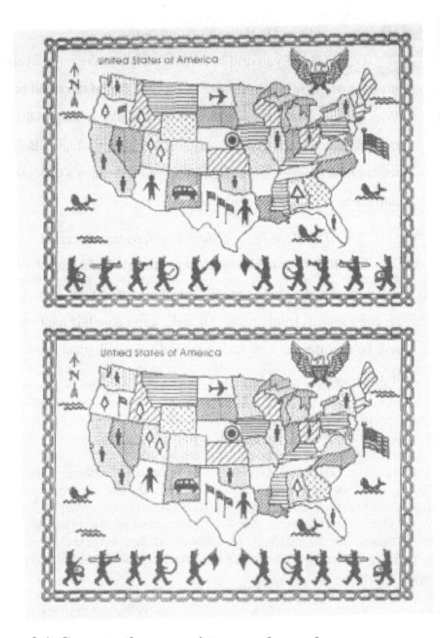

Figure 2-1. Compare these two pictures and record as many differences as you can find. Keep track of the time it takes you

to find each difference.

This test nicely simulates all sorts of processes in which differences are detected, including the process of software testing. For instance, I often use such twin pictures to simulate testing processes for software engineers. Once we separate out the fault location process, what we call "testing" is detecting differences between software requirements (written or unwritten) and software performance.

If a large number of people "test" a pair of pictures such as Figure 2-1, they do not all find the same differences in the same order. In a recent workshop, I had 47 people perform this experiment. No two found the differences in the same order. It's from observations such as this that people conclude that there's no order, or system, to software testing, and particularly to software failure detection.

There is order, however, but we must look at the data in a different way. If we gloss over which differences are found, and instead plot how many are found in how much time, we find a great consistency among people. Figure 2-2 shows this order in the form of a curve plotting the percentage of differences found versus time. I call this curve the Failure Detection Curve, because it is a universal description of the process of discovering differences — or, in software terms, failures.

41

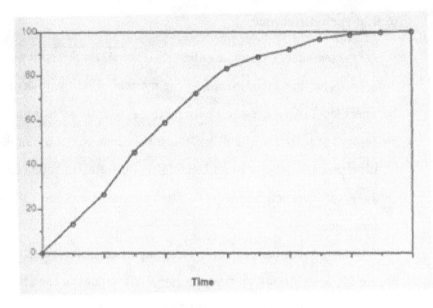

Figure 2-2. The rate of finding differences between the paired pictures shows remarkable consistency over a great diversity of people, yielding an S-curve.

As it turns out, of course, the Failure Detection Curve is exactly parallel to Root and Drew's observations about the discovery of oil fields. The easiest oil fields to find are found first, and so are the easiest picture differences. After the easy oil fields or picture differences have been found, the harder ones are left to find. We could paraphrase Root and Drew and give a description of Figure 2-1 by saying:

"First, the smallest amount of the test time is spent on a few easy problems; and second, most of the easy problems are found early in the test cycle."

This is the Difference Detection Dynamic.

2.1.2 Why we misestimate failure detection

In Figure 2-3, I have labeled the time intervals of the Failure Detection Curve to indicate the tautological nature of the Difference Detection Dynamic:

1. Failures are not equally easy to detect.

2. The easiest (shortest time) failures, by definition, will be detected first.

3. The hardest (longest time) failures, by definition, will be detected last.

4. Therefore, the average detection time will keep rising throughout the project.

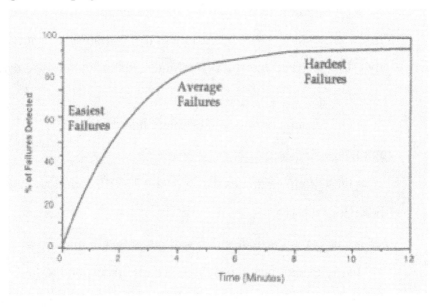

Figure 2-3. The Failure Detection Curve is a tautology, because

the failures that are hardest to find are found last. That's what "hardest to find" means.

This selection fallacy explains why testing seems to get harder and harder as it progresses. And that's one of the reasons so many projects lose their schedules in "testing," when things are "99% complete" for month after month. Figure 2-4 shows the results of an estimating exercise based on the paired pictures. First, I tell the participants that there are exactly 16 differences. At the end of two minutes, I ask them to estimate how long it will take them to find all remaining differences. The average estimate is right around 4 minutes, which corresponds closely to a linear projection of their experience so far.

At 4 minutes, I ask them to estimate again, and again they use a linear projection—which takes them to 6 minutes. At 6 minutes, they estimate 10 minutes. At 10 minutes, the group tends to divide in three:

• One group continues to estimate that they are "99% complete.

• One group estimates that they are "100% complete (and that I lied about the 16).

• One group estimates that will never be complete.

In my experience, these three groups correspond to personality types that exist in all real projects. In real projects, of course, nobody could truly know how many failures are yet to be detected, but managers can always find someone to give them the answer they want—once the project has been 99% complete for a few months.

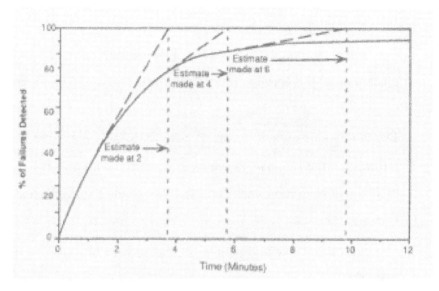

Figure 2-4. At each moment in the detection process, estimators tend to use a linear projection of their most current experience.

2.1.3 The bad news about the failure detection curve

The Failure Detection Curve is a characteristic curve of all failure detection technologies, such as,

- desk checking by the developer
- desk checking by some other person
- technical reviews by the inspection technique
- technical reviews by the walkthrough technique

45

- hand-generated test sets
- machine-generated test sets
- beta testing by selected customers
- field testing by thousands of customers
- "random" tests

Each technology has a curve of this same shape. The exact placement of the curve will different for different technologies, but there will always be that long, long, long, tail for "the last failure." The tail explains why the correct answer to "how many more failures are there?" always seems to be "One"—no matter how many have been removed. The bad news in the Failure Detection Curve is that:

There is no testing technology that detects failures in a linear manner.

But there is also good news. Although each technology has the same shape curve, each technology has different "easiest" and "hardest" failures to detect. Just like humans looking at the two pictures, no two testing processes will detect failures in exactly the same order. That provides the good news:

Combining different detection technologies creates an improved technology.

Figure 2-5 shows what happens to the Failure Detection Curve when we combine two technologies—such as adding technical reviews to machine testing, or using two beta testers instead of one. The combined curve has to be better than either of the individual curves. Unfortunately, no matter how you add them together, the combined curve still has the long tail of a Failure Detection Curve. That means it represents a natural dynamic, and we'll have to find ways to live with its tail.

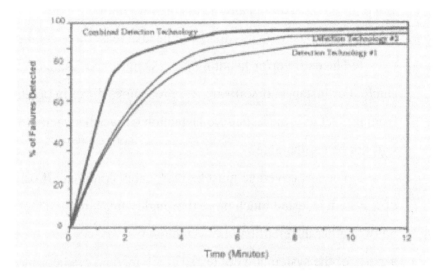

Figure 2-5. The sum of two Failure Detection Curves is another Failure Detection Curve, which will be better as long as the two failure detection technologies are not identical.

2.2. Living With the Failure Detection Curve

The Failure Detection Curve is a limiting condition of software engineering. like the Size/Complexity Dynamic. You can do worse than it says, but you can't do better. Pattern 1 and 2 organizations often do much worse than the Failure Detection

47

Curve would allow, which would be bad enough, but they also continue to predict that they can do much better. Thus, the discrepancy between what their promise and delivery grows larger.

2.2.1 The Failure Detection Curve as predictor

Pattern 3 organizations learn how to use the Failure Detection Curve to predict future patterns of software failure. In order for these predictions to be possible, you need at least three conditions:

1. The entire error-handling process must be reasonably stable. For instance, if software test procedures differ in practice from project to project, Failure Detection Curves between projects will not be comparable.

2. The test coverage must be reasonably complete. If one part of a system is tested much more thoroughly than another, there will be two rather different Failure Detection Curves, not one. If certain aspects of the system are not tested at all, then no prediction can be made about their future failure history.

3. The software pattern must take a systems engineering attitude towards failures, not a moral attitude. The systems engineering attitude considers failure rate, mean time between failures, or other failure measurements as parameters to be traded with other parameters such as cost, schedule, and functionality to deliver maximum value to customers. The moral attitude considers failures as signs of personal decay, and thus must insist on "zero defects." There is no way a Failure Detection Curve can predict the

moment of zero failures. It can, on the other hand, predict finite failure levels—such as when you will reach a certain mean time between failures—with reasonable precision, if the conditions of stability and diversity are met.

Given the conditions required, such predictions are not really available to Pattern 2 organizations. Their process tends to be unstable in just those projects where schedule prediction is desired, and those very projects cannot exert reliable control over their test coverage. And, in many Process 2 organizations, the moral attitude toward failure prevents them from improving the situation by small increments.

2.2.2 Undermining test coverage

For the Failure Detection Curve to be useful as an estimating device, test coverage must be reasonably complete. Intelligent planning is necessary to produce adequate test coverage, but intelligent planning is not sufficient. Several phenomena tend to destroy even the best planned test coverage.

Blocking faults. Here's an example of a blocking fault.

The Common Ordinary Works for Software (COWS) was running late on delivery of release 9.0 of their dairy herd management software (DHMS). Everyone in the testing lab was under a lot of pressure to get their test scripts executed and the STIs back to the developers for resolution.

Unfortunately, release 9.0 of DHMS contained a new data base interface routine which was supposed to allow the product to be sold to customers owning a wide variety of disk drives. The data base interface routine was delivered to the test lab on time, but didn't work very well. Indeed, it prevented many functions of the system from being tested effectively for seven weeks.

In the COWS situation, there are, in effect, two different parts of the system, the part to which access is blocked by the faulty data base interface routine and the part that isn't. In this situation, the Failure Detection Curve actually looked like Figure 2-6. This not the failure detection curve the management was expecting, but a sum of two curves, one for the unblocked part that started on time, and one for the blocked part that started seven weeks later.

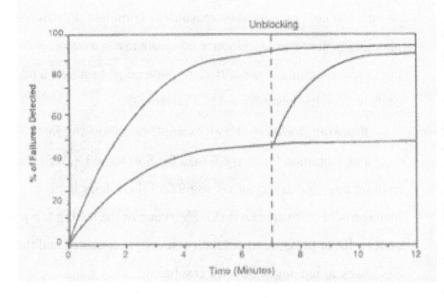

Figure 2-6. The Failure Detection Curve in a blocking situation does not follow the expected upper curve, but follows the lower curve, which is the sum of two curves, one of which only begins to rise after access to certain failures is unblocked .

If estimated completion time were based on the assumption that test coverage was uniform over the entire test period, the upper curve in the figure would have been used, and the predictions would have been far off. They would be at least seven weeks off for the late start, but that's not all. The atmosphere of growing pressure and frustration led to all sorts of shortcutting of the prescribed test procedures, resulting in an even slower test process and incomplete test coverage.

Masking faults. Masking faults are similar to blocking faults in producing the effects shown in Figure 2-6. The difference is that management—Pattern 3 management, at least—can take action to unblock a blocking fault and/or work around it as soon as they become aware of its existence. In the case of masking faults, management may never become aware of its existence, as in the following example:

After COWS delivered finally delivered release 9.0, things seemed to be going quite well. A few STIs came in from the field, but nothing extraordinary. Four months later, however, a flood of STIs crashed through the doors. Every new function in the system

51

seemed to be full of faults, but nobody in development could figure out why, if things were so bad, they hadn't heard earlier.

Management created a team to investigate the situation. What they discovered was that the packaging department had not received the new manuals on time, so had shipped release 9.0 without manuals. Customers were able to use their release 8.0 manuals, but had no systematic way to become aware of the new features of release 9.0. When the release 9.0 manuals finally arrived, customers started using the new features—or at least trying to use them—and started experiencing failures.

In effect, COWS depended on their customers to finish their failure location process, but parts of the system were masked from the customers until their new manuals arrived. Those parts were, therefore, blocked psychologically by a fault in the shipping procedure as effectively as if they had been blocked physically by a fault in the data base interface routine.

Late releases to test. Pattern 2 organizations are distinguished by their orderly process plans for assembling large systems out of smaller modules. In the course of events, however, some of the modules are not completed according to plan and thus are released late to the testing process. The testers may respond by stretching the schedule, but this is seldom allowed by management. Instead, the time planned for test coverage of late modules is reduced. To do the same amount of testing in less time, you must either go faster (and perhaps miss failures, or mis-record them) or truncate the tests themselves. In either case, late arriving modules violate the assumption of equal test coverage of all parts of the system.

2.2.3. Late finishing modules

Why are modules released late to test? Of course, there could be a number of reasons, but most of them are released late because the developer was having trouble reaching an acceptable level of unit test.

A cycle of poor coding. In many cases, the developer is caught in a positive feedback loop such as shown in Figure 2-7. Perhaps starting with a poor design or poor understanding of the problem, the developer writes some code which is not very clean. The uncleanliness of the code makes it difficult to work with, so that corrections have a high probability of making it even dirtier. This creates a cycle of patching and then patching to patches—a cycle that might be ended by scrapping the design and starting over, but more likely by management pressure to hand over the code to testing.

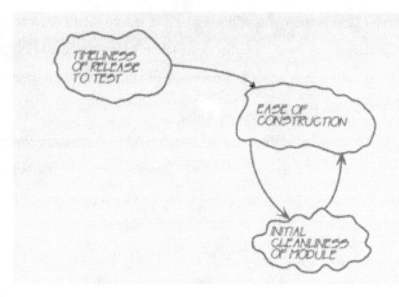

Figure 2-7. If the coding of a module gets off on the wrong foot, its subsequent correction may lead to a positive feedback loop that makes it even worse.

Fault-prone modules. In 1970, Gary Okimoto and I studied the history of faults in many releases of the IBM OS/360 operating system and discovered the existence of fault-prone modules. These modules accounting for less than 2% of the code in OS/360, but over their life had contributed over 80% of the faults. 1970 was in the midst of the structured programming movement, so we attempted to explain the existence of these modules in terms of weak control structures, such as GOTO statements. Our assumption was that these modules had been poorly coded to begin with.

We had limited success in our search, but people continued to notice the fault-prone phenomenon all over the world. Recently, we have begun to realize that in most cases, fault-prone modules are modules that for one reason or another never received their planned test coverage. And most of these were late releases—or not released at all—to test. Of course, if they were not full of faults when they were released to test, the lack of test coverage wouldn't matter. As indicated in Figure 2-8, fault-prone modules are the result of at least two factors—test coverage and initial uncleanliness.

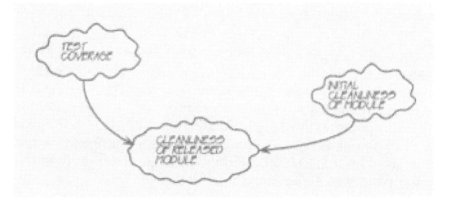

Figure 2-8. To create a released fault-prone module, you must have an unclean module to begin with, and you must fail to give it adequate test coverage.

The management decision point. The dynamics of Figures 2-7 and 2-8 are related, and can be put together to create the diagram of effects shown in Figure 2-9. This diagram shows that test coverage and cleanliness are not independent, but that the nature of their dependence is a result of management decision. In the diagram, we show the typical Pattern 2 management decision:

"Don't worry if we're behind schedule; we'll make it up in testing."

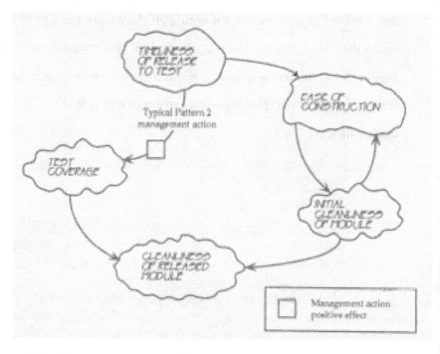

Figure 2-9. The dynamic created by the Pattern 2 management slogan, "Don't worry if we're behind schedule; we'll make it up in testing."

Pattern 2 managers hope to make up the schedule on poor modules by "getting lucky" in test, but the diagram of effects shows that just the opposite tends to happen. Late modules tend to be fault-prone modules—or, if you like, "unlucky" modules. Cutting or squeezing their test coverage ensures that they will remain "unlucky" when they go out the door.

Pattern 3 managers, understanding this dynamic, don't count on "luck." They understand that late delivery of a module to test gives them information about the cleanliness of that module. Therefore, they reverse the Pattern 2 decision and insist on giving that module greater test coverage, not less.

"Bad luck" estimating. The Pattern 2 manager compounds this problem by making predictions of test progress based on the original schedule. Figure 2-10 shows the Failure Detection Curve based on four modules, A-D, of equal cleanliness being introduced sequentially to the testing process.

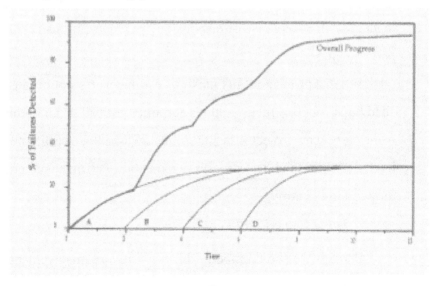

Figure 2-10. With an orderly sequence of modules introduced

**into testing and uniform cleanliness of modules, overall
progress in failure detection can be used to estimate test
completion.**

If the assumption of equal cleanliness holds true, the
composite curve of Figure 2-10 can be used to track the project's
progress on its schedule. But we've just seen that late-delivered
modules are more likely to be fault-prone, so a better picture of the
situation might be that of Figure 2-11.

Manager who use Figure 2-10 to make predictions of failure
detection progress will feel "unlucky" when actual experience is
more like the curve of Figure 2-11. As long as these managers
attribute this experience to luck, they will remain stuck in Pattern
2, because the first step towards Pattern 3 management is always
management acceptance of responsibility for poor project
performance.

When a project doesn't make its estimates, it's not because of
"bad bugs" or "bad luck," and it's certainly not bad programmers or
bad testers. The project was either managed badly, or estimated
badly, or both. In either case, it's responsibility of management. As
they say in the army,

> *There's no bad soldiers; there's only bad officers.*

Perhaps we should modify this for software management:

> *There's no bad managers; there's only managers who don't*

understand the dynamics of failure.

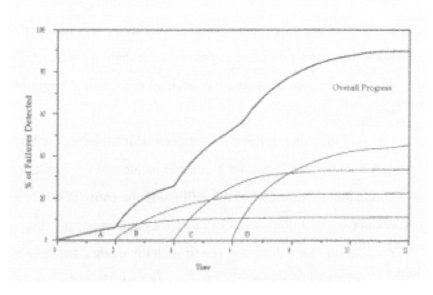

Figure 2-11. When management decisions mean that late modules are likely to be fault-prone modules, the Failure Detection Curve is likely to be stretched out much worse than it could be, leading to seriously optimistic estimates of failure detection progress.

2.3. Helpful Hints and Suggestions

• Not all failures are created equal. Therefore, one way to beat the Failure Detection Curve is to create a testing process that correlates the earliest failures with the most important failures. For instance, faults in deeply embedded routines on which other routines depend are likely to block more testing than less deep routines, so a testing process that scours these routines first may have increased favorable impact on the schedule. Similarly, test scripts that are based on actual customer usage will have a more favorable impact on customer acceptance than mathematically generated test scripts that cover all logical cases regardless of their value to customers.

• If there is a correlation between which failures are hardest to detect and which faults are hardest to locate and resolve, this would add to the effect of misestimating the entire detect-locate-resolve cycle. I don't know of any hard data supporting this correlation, but it does seem to fit with my clients' experience.

• The Failure Detection Curve can be S-shaped, as in Figure 2-2, or without the little curve at the beginning, as in Figure 2-3. The curve at the beginning is "startup time," and will be found to the extent that the testing activity is new to the organization. In an experienced organization that has put many projects through the same test procedures, the tail disappears.

• Of course, the Difference Detection Dynamic is not the only set of effects that influence the time to locate failures. That's why there are other explanations as to why the correct answer to "how many more failures are there?" always seems to be "One"—no matter how many have been removed. For instance, any dynamic that results in new faults being added to a system will stretch out the Failure Detection Curve, as will any process that slows down the error-handling process generally.

2.4 Summary

1. Failure detection is dominated by the tautology that the easiest failures to detect are the first failures to detect, so that as detection proceeds, the work gets harder, producing a characteristic Failure Detection Curve with a long tail.

2. The long tail of the Failure Detection Curve is one of the principal reasons managers misestimate failure detection tasks.

3. Because the Failure Detection Curve represents a natural dynamic, there is nothing we can do to perform better than it says. We can, however, perform much worse, if we're not careful of how we manage the failure detection process.

4. The Failure Detection Curve is not all bad news. The pattern of detected failures over time can be used as a predictor of the time to reach any specified level of failure detection, as long as nothing is happening to undermine test coverage.

5. Some of the things that can undermine test coverage are blocking faults, masking faults, and late releases to test.

6. Late finishing modules may arise from a cycle of poor coding, which means that they are more likely to be fault-prone modules. Management policies designed to speed testing of late finishing modules may actually make the problem worse, and may account for much so-called "bad luck" estimating.

2.5. Practice

1. Gather data on modules in a project you have available to study. For each module, record when it was delivered to testing compared with when it was originally scheduled to be delivered to testing. Also record the number of failures recorded in its testing, as well as the number of faults, if available. If the failure/fault history after delivery is available, record that, too. Then produce a study correlating delivery to test with various measures of module cleanliness.

2. Give a feasible explanation of how fault-prone modules could also have the property of concealing faults—that is, making them harder to uncover in normal testing. Then show the impact of this property on predictions of failure detection progress.

3. Give an example of a blocking fault from your experience. What was done to minimize the impact of blocking on the schedule? With the wisdom of hindsight, what could have been done?

4. Give an example of a masking fault from your experience. What finally stripped off the mask? What could have been done to strip off the mask earlier?

2.6 Chapter Appendix

Official Differences Between the Pair of Pictures in Figure 2-1

1. "Untied States" instead of "United States."

2. On the right border of #2, one ribbon weaves over rather than under, like the rest.

3. In the left-hand band, one drummer has no drumstick.

4. The flags in the two pictures have different numbers of stripes.

5. One eagle looks left, the other looks right.

6. In #2, the bottom straight border touches the woven border.

7. Virginia is dotted differently in the two pictures.

8. Iowa is striped differently in the two pictures.

9. One border is missing between New Hampshire and Vermont.

10. The persons in Oklahoma are different sizes in the two pictures.

11. The trees in Alabama are different.

12. The N arrows are different in the two pictures.

13. The Southwest corner of Missouri is missing in one picture.

14. The flag in Oregon is reversed.

15. Long Island, New York is missing in one picture.

16. In New Mexico, one van touches the Texas border and one doesn't.

Chapter 3: Locating The Faults Behind The Failures

"...complex systems will evolve from simple systems much more rapidly if there are stable intermediate forms than if there are not. The resulting complex forms in the former case will be hierarchic."- Herbert A. Simon

Quite possibly the hardest part of error-handling is fault location. Pattern 2 organizations seldom realize how much effort they are putting into fault location because they lump it with some other activity. Some lump fault location with failure detection under the title "testing." Others lump it with fault resolution under "debugging," although that title is also used for all three activities, detection, location, and resolution.

Pattern 3 organizations, however, examine their processes more carefully, and know that the most troublesome and time-consuming error-handling activity is tracking each failure back to the fault that is its progenitor. Sometimes the relation between failure and fault is obvious, but when it's not, extremely long delays can result—often for reasons we'll develop in this chapter.

3.1 The Dynamics of Fault Location

Figure 3-1 shows figures for three typical clients who measured fault location as distinct from failure detection. The three pie charts show the relative amount of effort each spent detecting failures, locating faults, and resolving them. (Of course, these figures still exclude the unrecognized prevention and distribution activities, which may be even larger.) Location time was the biggest recognized expenditure for all three. Why does this happen?

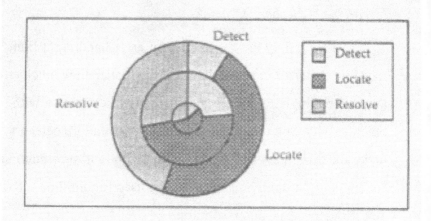

Figure 3-1. Typical software organizations spend as much effort on fault location as they do on detection and repair together.

3.1.1 Direct effects of system size

In an earlier volume, we saw the Fault Detection Dynamic which is a special case of the Size/Complexity Dynamic

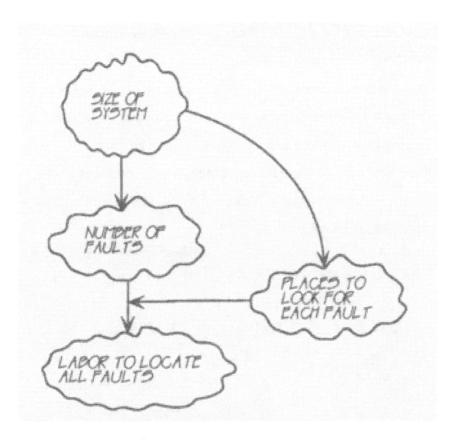

Figure from *How Software is Built*. The source of complexity in the Size/Complexity Dynamic applied to the problem of finding faults in a system. If your development process creates faults at the same rate, your larger system will contain more faults. Since the system is bigger, there are more places to look for each fault. Thus, total fault location labor grows non-linearly. This is called the Fault Location Dynamic.

In a given software cultural pattern, the cleanliness of

67

individual parts remains in a more or less constant range. Therefore, as the number of parts increases, there are more faults. When there is a failure and we have to look for one of these faults, we have more places to look, so the time to look is longer. Thus, the time spent locating all faults grows at least as fast as the square of the size, because there are more faults and more places to look (Figure 3-2). Several consequences of this dynamic are clear in the organizations I have studied.

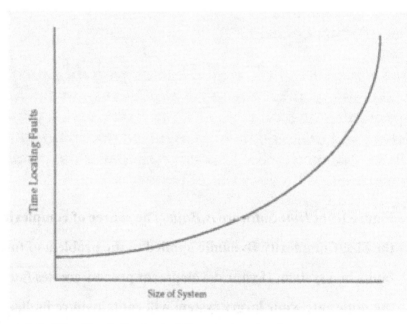

Figure 3-2. The Fault Location Dynamic: As the system grows larger, the time to locate the source of problems grows non-linearly.

3.1.2 Divide and Conquer to beat Size/Complexity

The Size/Complexity Dynamic also has less direct effects on the time to locate faults. In order to beat the dynamic, software engineers adopt the strategy of "Divide and Conquer." A numerical example of the reasoning goes like this:

1. Suppose the system size is 1000 units.

2. By the Square Law, this would produce labor proportional to 1000^2, or 1,000,000.

3. We divide the system into 10 parts, of 100 units each.

4. Each 100 unit part requires labor proportional to 100^2, or 10,000.

5. There are 10 units, so total labor is proportional to 10 x 10,000, or 100,000.

6. Thus, by dividing in this way, we have reduced total labor by a factor of 10.

Of course, this reasoning makes certain optimistic assumptions. In practice we don't achieve quite this good a result. As indicated in Figure 3-3, although we reduce the labor per part, we add a new source of labor, the labor to integrate the parts. It's this integration labor that prevents us carrying the Divide and Conquer argument to its outrageous limit, which would suggest building a million lines of code by dividing the system into a million modules!

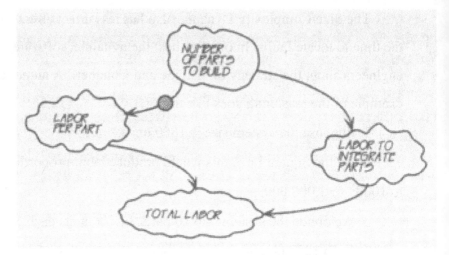

Figure 3-3. In an attempt to beat the Size/Complexity Dynamic, we resort to a variety of process improvements. The major tactic is "Divide and Conquer."

The actual decision on how many parts to create is a complex design problem, but the gross dynamics of the problem are easy to understand if we express them graphically as in Figure 3-4. Total effort is part-building effort plus integration effort. Both of these components are non-linear functions of the number of parts. They move in opposite directions, so as we gain in one, we lose in the other. Somewhere between one big part and a million little ones, we find the optimal division that minimizes total labor to solve the problem.

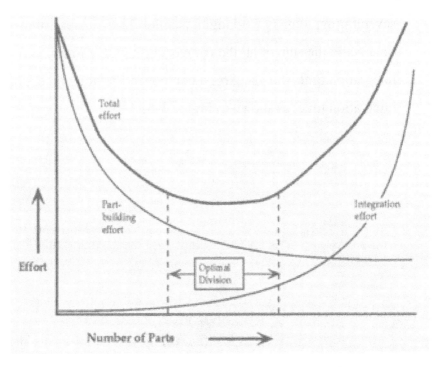

Figure 3-4. The more parts we divide the system into, the more linear the labor of each part becomes. On the other hand, the more parts, the more integration effort grows non-linearly. Eventually, there would be so many small parts that the integration effort is greater than the building effort.

3.1.3 Divide the labor to beat delivery time

From a software engineering view, however, the Divide and Conquer strategy has another component. If we had all the time in the world, we would allow one programmer to apply Divide and Conquer to each project. In order to get done faster, however, we may decide not just to divide the work, but to divide it among

71

several programmers working in parallel. Then, instead of the total time being the sum of all the component-building times, plus integration time, it is the largest component-building time, plus integration time, as shown in Figure 3-5.

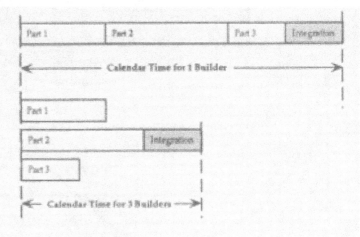

Figure 3-5. By putting several people to work, we can reduce the overall calendar time to build a system. This figure assumes total integration time is the same in both cases.

Figure 3-5 shows that dividing the problem and dividing the responsibilities are two different tactics, each with its own effects. Dividing the problem tends to reduce the total work, because it beats the Square Law. Dividing the responsibilities reduces the total calendar time, because it uses resources in parallel. But neither of them has to work at all, unless the process is controlled properly.

3.1.4 Indirect effects of system size

In dividing the problem, we have to control the design so that we don't lose the advantage we gain by adding so much integration work. In dividing the responsibilities, we have to control the process so that we don't lose the advantage we gain by adding so much process work. Process work is added because of necessity to coordinate among different people. Figure 3-6 shows how the process overhead adds both to the calendar time and the total labor. It always costs more to have more people working on a project, but it may be faster.

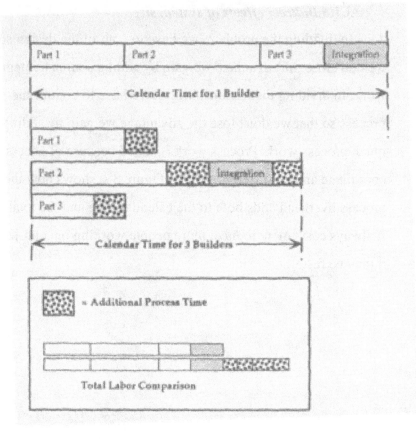

Figure 3-6. More realistically, however, the more people, the more process time caused by coordination problems among the people, in addition to integration effort between the models. This additional process time means losing some of the savings in calendar time, and also spending more total labor.

In order for the division of responsibilities to fulfill its promise of faster completion, it must be well managed. As usual, to manage it well, you need to understand the dynamics. Figure 3-7

shows four kinds of additional work that division of
responsibilities creates that impact the time to locate faults:

- STI circulation time

- process errors

- administrative burden

- political time

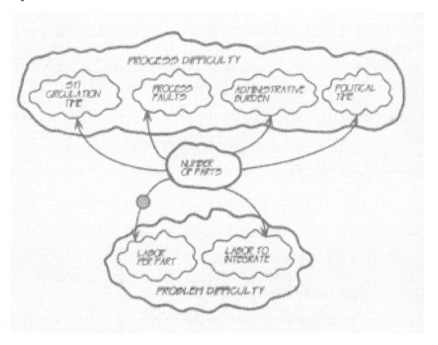

**Figure 3-7. As we divide and conquer, we not only add
integration effort, but we create a more complex process.**

The dynamics of each of these demonstrates a way we can
lose the benefits of Divide and Conquer through process
complexity and poor control. We shall look at each in turn,

especially to see how they may indicate it's time for a Pattern 2 organization to think seriously about what it will take to move to Pattern 3 in order to cope with increasing problem demands.

3.2 Circulation of STIs Before Resolution

Suppose we receive an STI that stems from a code fault. If it is to be resolved by changing code, it must eventually reach the hands of a person responsible for the code in which the repair will be made. If there were only one programmer, this would be no problem. With more people, however, each is responsible for only a part of the whole. The situation becomes a sensitive test of the organization's software culture. As systems grow larger, STIs no longer tend to be handled by the first person who sees them. In an organization under the stress of increasing customer and problem demands, many STIs cycle around from desk to desk, some for months, or years.

3.2.1. The Resolver Location Time (RLT)

An easy measurement to use here is the time between receipt of an STI and the time the eventual solver receives it. Even if there is no SFA database, this measure is easy to determine from almost any sort of routing slip. It is the time to locate the right person to solve the problem—which we may call the "resolver location time"—or RLT. Here's an example of a routing slip showing what time each person received the STI:

John 10/10/8am

Mary 10/12/4pm

Paul 10/13/9am

John 10/13/2pm

Joan 10/17/11am

The STI first arrived in the office at 8am on 10/10, and after a circuitous route, found its way to Joan at 11am on 10/17. Joan must have resolved the issue because hers is the last name on the slip. Therefore, the time to reach the resolver is the difference between the first and last times, or 7 days and 3 hours. The RLT doesn't say anything about how long Joan took to resolve the STI, only the time to reach her, and can thus be quite different from the "incident resolution time"—or IRT—which does depend on how long Joan took.

If the average RLT starts to grow—or the longest RLT starts to grow—something is breaking down. Pattern 3 organizations routinely monitor the distribution of RLTs, because they are sensitive indicators of loss of control. The RLT doesn't necessarily tell you why control is breaking down—it might be the code, or it might be the way in which the STI is being handled—but the distribution of these times will give a clue as to where to look further. In any case, a rising mean or maximum RLT is a sign for early management action.

3.2.2. The dynamics of STI circulation

Figure 3-8 shows some of the dynamics of STI circulation. Because of the Size/Complexity dynamic, organizations are more likely to experience the non-linearity of this effect as they attempt to solve bigger problems. With more total faults, there will be more STIs circulating. With a bigger system, even without the circulation effect there would be more time to locate faults. In other words, problem demands get you off to a worse start, and once you are behind, it's hard to catch up.

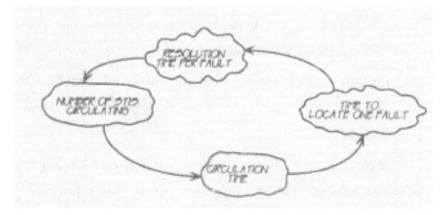

Figure 3-8. The circulation dynamic used for the simulation model of Figure 3-9.

Because of this dynamic, uncontrolled STI circulation is an easy way to spot a Pattern 2 organization feeling the push of growing problem demands. Initially, the circulation feeds on the number of faults produced, so if the organization doesn't improve the cleanliness of individual modules, they'll be sucked into this

78

maelstrom as the number of modules per system expands.

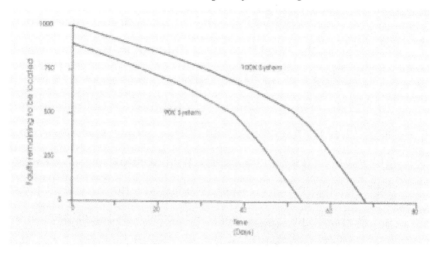

Figure 3-9 shows the results of a teaching simulation based on Figure 3-8 which shows the effect of system size on this circulation problem. Figure 3-9 shows the time to clean up all the outstanding STIs in two systems, one with 90,000 lines of code and one with 100,000 lines of code. Because STI's circulate, the time to locate all STI's in a system grows even faster than the square of the system size, even if the time to fix an STI is zero. (In this simulation, an 11 per cent increase in the system size led to a 28 per cent increase in the time to locate the last STI.)

There's an instructive story behind this model:

YES Systems was a third party software developer. The original 90K project had been bid, sold, and was well under way when the project lead was asked by his manager to add 10K of new function. In estimating how much additional time to ask for, the project lead increased the fault location time by 11%, from 53 working days to 60, an 11% increase.

Later, YES asked me to help them figure out why the total project had been 4 months late. We developed some diagrams of effects to teach the management what went wrong. Then we put their own numbers into some rough simulations for fault location.

This simulation modeled pre-release testing efforts for a first release, and assumed (far too optimistically, of course) that no new faults are introduced when correcting the ones located and that located faults are resolved instantly. The model assumed 10 faults per 1000 lines of code (10 F/KLOC) going into pre-release testing, based on YES's previous experience on similar systems. The model also assumed exactly one STI per fault (which was very optimistic). The larger system thus starts with 11% more code, 11% more faults and generates 11% more STIs. But, of course, it takes much more than 11% longer to find al of them.

In this case, 69 work days are needed instead of the 60 that the project lead predicted on the basis of the 90,000 line system. Because there were about 3 to 5 programmers involved in location activities at any moment, the model proposed that two or three weeks of the lateness was just because of size and circulation effects. Actual measurements showed that fault location took approximately 75 days (and did not actually remove all faults).

We then asked the question, "How much cleaner code would YES have to produce to negate the effect of an 11% increase in system size?" In order to have matched the time of the 90,000 line system, the entire 100,000 line system would have to have been written with no more than 7 F/KLOC. This was an unlikely improvement over YES's normal experience, and showed they would have to make some significant changes in their development process to compensate for increased problem demand.

One of the interesting effects of this simulation was that it motivated YES to make some measurements. They discovered that the late-added 10K actually showed a discovered fault rate of 17 F/KLOC, almost double their usual experience. This was the first time they had an actual measure of how much poorer their code was when written fast, under pressure.

This kind of rough simulation is very different in motive than the kind of precise simulation that a Pattern 4 organization might run to optimize their operations. The purpose here was educational, helping a Pattern 2 organization learn what sorts of changes they needed to transform themselves into Pattern 3.

3.3 Process Faults: Losing STIs

In Pattern 2 organizations losing the battle with customer and problem demands, STIs don't just circulate, they get "lost." Some get lost forever. People hope they will go away. Perhaps simply getting STIs off their desks will make them disappear.

Losing STI's may be a conscious reaction to overload, or it may be unconscious, as the following story illustrates:

At First Federal Fidelity Financial , each STI was represented by a dump averaging half an inch thick. One programmer, Emery, had a stack of dumps next to his desk approximately 7 feet tall, thus containing about 170 unfinished STIs. (This was about average, apparently, as they had 40 programmers and something over 6,000 STIs, though they weren't really sure how many, as their data base had broken down.)

When I asked Emery how he decided which dump to work on next, he explain that he used a "first-in-first-out" method. He knew he could never handle all the STIs, so he felt that this was the "fair" way to proceed. When he received an STI, he placed it on top of the stack. When he finished one, he took his next one from the bottom.

This seemed fair enough until I observed what Emery did when he received a call from one of the loan executives asking about one of the STIs in the middle of the stack. After much awkward fumbling, Emery managed to locate the dump about a foot from the bottom of the stack. He looked at it a bit, explained some of the problems to the executive on the phone, and replaced the dump—on top of the stack.

When I questioned him about this procedure, Emery seemed genuinely unaware of what he had done. He was shocked to discover that his "fair" system had the effect of punishing anyone who happened to inquire about the status of their STI. In fact, you don't need a simulation to see that if you inquired often enough, your STI would never get out of the stack. It would be, in effect, "lost" in the system—circulating forever, like the Flying Dutchman.

3.4 Political Time: Status Walls

The problem of getting an STI into the right hands is not merely a matter of awareness and logic. In the culture of most large organizations, there is a status hierarchy that tends to obstruct the simple logic of fault location. For example, the programmers who work on the operating system often have a higher status than those who work on applications.

When an STI arrives that doesn't obviously go in one place or another, it tends to get bumped quickly to the lowest status group that can imaginably be responsible. In such an organization,

1. Operating system errors sometimes wind up in the applications area.

2. Application errors tend to wind up in the documentation group.

3. Documentation errors tend to get shipped back to the

customers with instructions to "use the system correctly."

Such an incorrect initial routing tends to add a constant delay to time to locate the fault, amplifying the effect we've already seen in the simulation. Unfortunately, the status hierarchy not only leads to initial misclassification, but creates strong walls of defense between areas. These walls grow stronger as the stress on a project grows, so it becomes very difficult to get a problem out of a wrong area once it has fallen in.

Of course, as the system grows more complex, many faults are the result of miscommunication between areas, and cannot truly be said to be in one area or the other. Moreover, they cannot be properly resolved without considering both areas. But as the status walls grow higher and stronger, it's hard to get the people together from the different areas to pinpoint these boundary problems, let alone to resolve them.

In some Pattern 2 organizations, the management attempts to accelerate the processing of STIs by keeping score on each group. They count the number of STIs being held by each group each week, and punish groups who keep can't keep their score down. To avoid blame, the idea is not to be caught with the "hot potato" at the end of the week. This leads to fast processing of STIs at each stop on their journey, but a long, long journey before they find their way home—another backwards effect of management intervention.

3.5 Labor Lost: Administrative Burden

In troubled Pattern 2 organizations, all this cycling plus the growing backlog swell the administrative burden on the developers. They spend little time actually resolving STIs, and more time:

• looking for lost STIs

• working with the wrong documentation for the particular STI

• answering queries about what happened to particular STIs

• complaining about the customers or the testers who generate STIs

• arguing so that they won't be blamed for STIs

• playing games like "hot potato" to beat the management measurement system.

All this work leaves them little time or appetite for truly important administrative work. For example, tracing each resolved fault back to all relevant STIs, so as to clear the STI data base, is important administrative work that only the developers can do. It reduces the size of the STI data base, and thus reduces both stress and further administrative burden.

This kind of administrative burden affects all programmer work, and particularly, adds to the average time to locate the true fault behind any failure. No wonder many organizations reach the point where they decide to handle their 10,000 outstanding STIs by scrapping the lot and starting over. In doing so, they relieve the pressures of circulating STIs, but if they don't get to the root cultural cause, they will soon have another 10,000 STIs circulating.

What they really need to do is sit down and ask, "What is this enormous load of circulating STIs trying to tell us about our culture?" Having obtained the answer, the next question should be, "What do we propose to do about it?"

3.6 Helpful Hints and Suggestions

• A handful of routing slips tabulated each week can adequately estimate RLT for the organization. The average number of stops on each slip also gives a good estimate of the level of "hot potato" being played.

• Considering the non-linear effects of circulating STIs, it's not a bad idea to scrap unresolved STIs as a first step in getting the organization back under control. This should be done systematically, however, and not just as an emotional response to actual collapse. A reasonable policy is that any STI not resolved in, say, two months is simply sent back to the originators. If they still care enough, they can just send it back. In my experience, the resubmission rate is less than 10%, although it may be low because people are disgusted with the programmers.

• If STIs are sent back to originators, it's a good idea to send them along with a polite note. For example, one of my clients uses this message:

After two months of effort, we have been unable to locate the fault that led to STI #99999 (attached). It is possible that this fault was resolved in processing a different STI, in which case, you won't experience it again.

If you wish, however, you may simply resubmit the STI. Of course, it would help us if you added any new information you may have discovered in the meantime. Please accept our apology for not being able to resolve this problem in a more decisive manner.

• Even though the underlying dynamics are the same, the kind of consulting advice an organization needs depends critically on their cultural pattern. Consider the case of circulating STIs:

1. If your organization is at the "7-foot stack of dumps" level of keeping track of STIs, the first thing you should do is notice that the Divide and Conquer strategy applies very nicely to stacks of dumps. As I suggested to Emery, two 3.5-foot stacks of dumps are much easier to search than one 7-foot stack. On the basis of that advice, he decided that I was a genius.

2. If your organization is at an automated database level of keeping track of STIs, one of the first things you should do is consider "groupware" which would allow any number of people to share the STI information at the same time. But the introduction of

groupware into Emery's organization could prove a disaster, as Emery would now have all 6,000 STIs to think about, not just the 170 stacked up by his desk. This illustrates an essential principle of culture change: You can't go from Stone Age tools to Space Age tools in one step.

3.7 Summary

1. System size has a direct effect on the dynamics of fault location, but there are indirect effects as well. We use divide and conquer to beat the Size/Complexity Dynamic, and we also divide the labor to beat delivery time. These efforts, however, lead to a number of indirect effects of system size on fault location time.

2. You can learn a great deal about its culture by observing how an organization handles its STIs. In particular, you can learn to what degree its cultural pattern is under stress of increased customer or problem demands.

3. An important dynamic describes the circulation of STIs, which grows non-linearly the more STIs are in circulation.

4. Process errors such as losing STIs also increase location time.

5. Political issues, such as status boundaries, can also contribute non-linearly to extending location time. Management action to reduce circulation time by punishing those who hold STIs can lead to the opposite effect.

6. In general, poorly controlled handling of STIs leads to an enlarged administrative burden, which in turn leads to less poorly controlled handling of STIs. When STIs get out of hand, management needs to study what information that gives them about their cultural pattern, then take action to get at the root causes, not merely the symptoms.

3.8. Practice

1. Draw a diagram of effects for the game of "hot potato" with STIs. One of the variables should be "average number of names on routing slips." Show how the management intervention could be changed to reverse this undesirable effect.

2. Show how increased customer demands—such as doubling or tripling the number of systems sold—affects STI circulation. In particular, incorporate the effect that each fault is found many times by multiple customers.

3. A field service staff—sometimes several levels—is often added to marketing to filter out some of the customers' STIs before they reach developers. Each level of field organization, however, tends to slow down the transit of an STI from the customer to the developers. The longer this delay, the more STIs are found for the same fault, while the customers wait for the organization to find it, resolve it, and distribute the fix. Use a diagram of effects to show how this delay effect limits the effectiveness of multi-level STI

filtering process.

Chapter 4: Fault Resolution Dynamics

"I hope they won't uglify the house," sighed Lady Laura. "People generally do when the try to improve a sweet, picturesque old place." - Mary Elizabeth Braddon, - *Miranda, Book II*

Substitute the word "program" for the word "place" and Lady Laura could have been a modern day software developer. It's one thing to detect failures and locate faults. When it comes to fixing those faults and actually producing an improvement, that's another kettle of fish—or, as the industry cliche has it, another bowl of spaghetti. Just as with sweet, picturesque old houses, as systems get older, they get more and more difficult to improve. Thus, a Pattern 2 organization that seems to have a stable customer environment can experience growing problem demands—the demands of keeping the sweet, picturesque old software working. In this chapter, we'll see some of the reasons this happens, and what they tell us about the organization's software culture.

4.1 Basic Fault Resolution Dynamics

4.1.1. Size/Complexity Dynamics

If the quality of individual parts is held constant, then as the number of parts increases, the time spent fixing problems grows at least as fast as the square of the size, because there are more faults and each fault takes longer to fix. This dynamic is very similar to location time dynamics.

Another effect similar to those discussed previously is the selection of easier problems to fix first. This may be unintentional, as when faults that are difficult to locate are also difficult to fix, or intentional, when programmers put aside tough problems in order to cope with time pressure. The effect of either type of selection is more or less the same—a prolongation of the time to resolve faults, well beyond any simple extrapolation of the faults removed so far.

These basic fault resolution dynamics are quite similar to the dynamics of detection and location because they don't yet take into account the way that resolution differs from detection and location —namely, that resolving a fault usually results in changes. And changes to code, like any new code, are subject to faults themselves. Not every "resolution" is an improvement.

4.1.2 Side Effects

The consideration of these faulty resolutions slows down the resolution process. As the system gets more complex, side effects —inadvertent changes to the code when correcting faults—grow more likely. Thus, when we fix one thing in a bigger system, there are more other things to consider. More things to consider means the Size/Complexity Dynamic comes into play, which means increased time to make fixes correctly, as shown in Figure 4-1.

But even when we take as much time as we like, nobody's perfect—least of all when writing programs. We could try to beat the dynamic of Figure 4-1 by ignoring possible side-effects, but that's no solution. As Figure 4-2 indicates, if we don't consider side effects carefully, we will feed new faults into the system through the fault correcting process, thus complicating and prolonging the work in a different way.

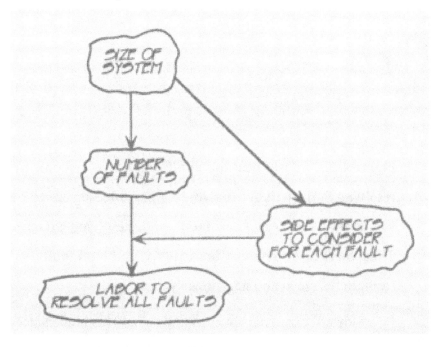

Figure 4-1. The Size/Complexity Dynamic applied to the problem of resolving faults in a system. If you create faults at the same rate, there are more faults. Since the system is bigger, there are more possible side effects to consider when resolving a fault. Thus, total fault resolution time grows nonlinearly.

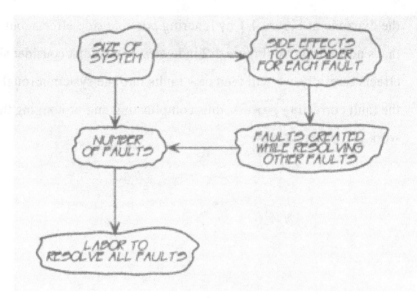

Figure 4-2. Can you beat the Size/Complexity Dynamic by resolving faults without considering possible side effects? If you do that, you create new faults while resolving old ones. Thus, there are even more faults to fix, and total fault resolution time grows non-linearly.

Side effects do not always show themselves immediately, nor do they always show as faults. Other side effects are increases (sometimes decreases) in code size, destruction of code quality, loss of design integrity, and documentation obsolescence. All these side effects lead to a decay of maintainability.

4.2 Fault Feedback Dynamics

The most obvious non-linear result of side effects is simply the creation of more faults to fix. Faults put into a system when attempting to correct other faults is called "fault feedback."

4.2.1 The Fault Feedback Ration (FFR)

The "fault feedback ratio" (FFR)—the number of problems created per "fix"—is a sensitive measure of a software culture. The formula for FFR is

FFR = faults created / faults resolved

FFR can be approximated historically by counting the number of faults that are found in code that was created as part of the resolution of an earlier fault. This approximation underestimates FFR (because there will be faults that haven't yet been located), but that doesn't diminish its usefulness.

Figure 4-3 shows the changes in FFR over time in a six-month project that was headed for serious trouble. Management noticed the growth in FFR and introduced "fix reviews" to remedy the situation. Because of the backlog of old, non-reviewed fixes, it took several weeks before the impact of this change started to show in the FFR. With the benefit of hindsight, management agreed that they should have instituted a retroactive review of all previous fixes. This insight showed they were on their way to Pattern 3 thinking.

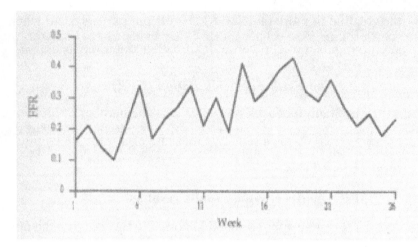

Figure 4-3. The fault feedback ratio (FFR) is a sensitive indicator of trouble in a project. In this project, management noticed the growth in FFR and introduced "fix reviews" to remedy the situation.

FFR is a critical parameter measuring the quality in any software organization. It's easily measured, it ought to be measured, yet it's seldom measured. When it is measured, we find that the average "fix" creates somewhere between 0.1 and 0.3 new problems. When it's not measured, the FFR is probably higher, for the cultures that need to measure are just the ones least likely to do any measuring.

4.2.2 The impact of FFR

Why is FFR so important? Figure 4-4 shows the results of a teaching simulation of the feedback of side effect faults. The first curve (finishing at 240) had an FFR of 0.3. The second (finishing after 480) had an FFR of 0.36, while the third FFR was 0.396.

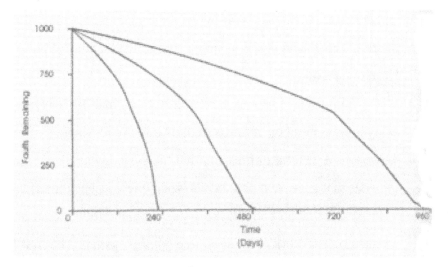

Figure 4-4. The time to finish removing faults is critically dependent on the fault feedback ratio. The two simulations differ only in their feedback ratios. A 20 per cent difference in feedback ratio leads to an 88 per cent difference in completion time, but the next 10 per cent increase leads to a 112 per cent increase.

The three curves show what can happen as FFR changes by small amounts when the organization's process has started to become unstable. And, of course, when the organization's process is becoming unstable, the fault feedback ratio generally increases by large amounts, not small amounts, so the effect is even worse.

4.2.3 Having an impact on FFR

The FFR is a sensitive indicator of the fault resolution process, summarizing a number of tangible and intangible attitudes and actions. This means that the manager who wishes to control the fault resolution process can use the FFR as a control point. Here's one example:

CompuBreakfast was suffering from an inability to clear away a large number of faults in their Integrated Menu System. There was a general impression that the system was like Hydra, the monster that grew two new heads when one was hacked off.

As the first step in attacking this problem, they did a bit of archaeological work on their source control system. The first figure they extracted was the average FFR, which was 0.36, which seemed rather high. Most organizations are able to improve such a figure very easily, with a few simple measures. For instance, they can conduct a brief technical review of each fix before putting it into the system.

When I returned for a second consulting visit, six weeks later, CompuBreakfast had not done anything about the review idea. I asked the Information Systems Manager what had happened, and he told me that after discussing the idea, his managers had rejected it because "reviewing such small changes was a waste of time."

I encouraged them to return to their archaeological work and plot the FFR against the size of each change, in lines of source code modified. This research produced the graph of Figure 4-5, which surprised them. They had predicted something quite different—as indicated by the straight line in the figure. The difference between the predicted and actual graphs convinced the managers that reviewing even a one-line change was not at all a "waste of time."

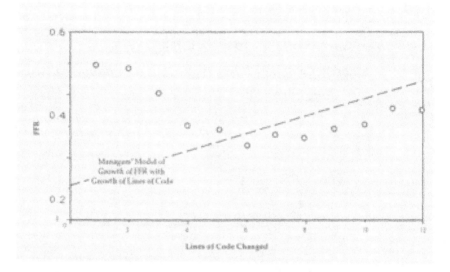

Figure 4-5. The organization believes FFR will increase linearly with the number of lines of code changed. In practice, very small fixes had larger feedback ratios.

The managers' prediction was linear: each line of code added proportionately to the difficulty of making a correct change. Thus, large changes would be difficult, but small changes would be "trivial." The actual behavior was non-linear: the difficulty of making a correct change was also influenced by the care taken by the programmers. That care, in turn, was affected by the perceived difficulty of the change, which in turn was influenced by the managers' own linear model—which said that small changes ought to be easier.

4.2.4 A self-invalidating model

Figure 4-6 shows the dynamic of how, in practice, this is a self-invalidating model:

> ***The belief that a change will be easy to do correctly makes it less likely that the change will be done correctly.***

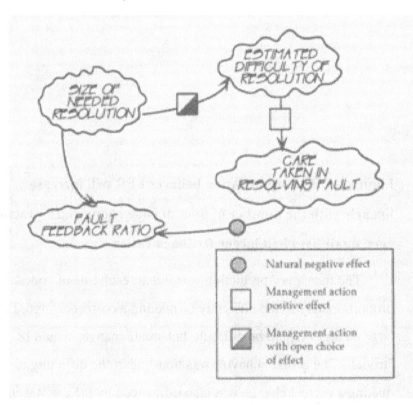

Figure 4-6. The organization's model that FFR will increase linearly with the number of lines of code changed creates a nonlinear dynamic that invalidates the model. Changing their belief system allowed the managers to mandate that all changes would be reviewed, even one-liners. This removed the programmer's model from the dynamic, and eventually produced an FFR curve that was much more linear with lines of code—and had a mean of 0.16, which made a noticeable improvement in the project's performance.

4.3 Deterioration Dynamics

Side effects lead to software of lower quality—the increased faults decrease the value to customers. The code may do the wrong thing. The code may do the right thing, but inefficiently. Even worse, it's not just the delivered quality that suffers, but the internal quality as well—the value of the code to developers. Over the life of a software system, this internal quality is more important than the external quality in determining its controllability.

4.3.1. Maintainability must be maintained

In time, existing code may even come to have negative quality, meaning that it would be cheaper to develop new code than attempt to keep repairing the old. Many Pattern 1 and Pattern 2 organizations are holding large inventories of negative quality software, but usually they are unaware of that fact. Or, if they are aware, they are so unsure of their ability to develop new code that they continue to limp along patching ever more pitiful and expensive systems.

They know they must patch, of course, because they know that any system must have its functions maintained. What they don't understand, however, is that any system must also have its maintainability maintained. Even software that is initially well designed and implemented begins to deteriorate and lose its maintainability in a software culture that doesn't regularly invest in maintainability.

What has to be maintained for maintainability to be preserved? Besides functional faults and loss of efficiency, other side effects are increases (or decreases) in size of the code itself, destruction of code quality, loss of design integrity, obsolescence of documentation. All of these together constitute the decay of maintainability, as indicated in Figure 4-7.

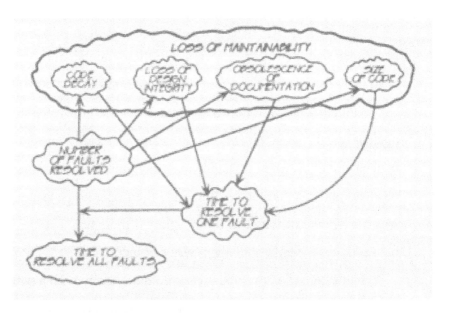

Figure 4-7. Side effects may not only show up in functional faults and inefficiencies, but also in terms of reduced maintainability, which makes it even harder to resolve future faults.

Quite likely, the loss of maintainability is the ultimate cause of "death" for even the best designed, built, and maintained systems.

4.3.2 The ripple effect

One measure of maintainability is through the "ripple effect," the number of separate code areas that have to be changed to affect a single fault resolution.

Some years ago, one hardware manufacturer studied this ripple effect of changes to their operating system and found that each change led to approximately 300 other changes. They concluded that the slightest decrease in their maintainability would have led to one change creating an infinite number of changes.

Mathematically, their operating system was equivalent to a nuclear reactor—one that was on the verge of turning into a nuclear bomb. Before that happened, they quit the mainframe business and discontinued maintaining their operating system. This was not a client of mine, so I don't know if there was a connection between these events. Perhaps it was a coincidence.

The ripple effect can be measured quite easily with a software tool used with the configuration control tool, and ought to be monitored by management to give them a glimpse of what is happening inside the code.

4.3.3 Destruction of black box design integrity

Where does this deterioration in maintainability come from? A typical cause is the gradual destruction of design integrity by pathological connections across module boundaries. Black box modules are pieces of code that

• can only be influenced through a known, bounded, input interface

• can only influence other code through a known, bounded, output interface.

Black box modules are a design technique for slowing the

Size/Complexity Dynamic for fault correction. Figure 4-8 shows how this happens. The more modular we make the system, the fewer side effects we need to consider. We trade for this effect by creating "modularity faults," or faults in the interfaces between modules. We never get something for nothing.

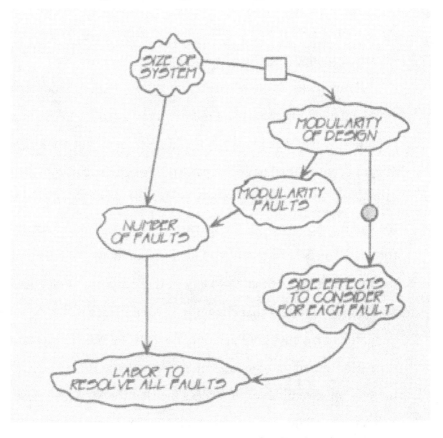

Figure 4-8. You can slow the Size/Complexity Dynamic on resolving faults by building in black box units of code. If your code units are truly black boxes, then the number of side

effects you have to consider when correcting a fault is greatly reduced, but you pay by creating the possibility of modularity faults, or interface errors. This is the Modular Dynamic.

Knowing how the Modular Dynamic works, we can also understand how it breaks down. When fixing some fault, the programmer sees a way to short-cut the solution by bypassing the known, bounded, interface, as in this example:

Jeremy was fixing an operating system fault in module WYA, deep in the calling tree. The fault involved a failure to consider condition X that was known at the highest level, but not known to WYA because it had not been passed through the calling sequences. The proper black box fix would have been to modify all the calling sequences on the way down to WYA, to include the flag for condition X. But this would have required considering and modifying all places that used any of those calling sequences.

Jeremy thought that changing several places would be more dangerous than changing just one. Besides, he was a bit pressed for time. He figured that the fault in WYA could be fixed by reaching directly up several levels to access the flag for X. Where necessary, WYA then reached back to the high level and modified the flag. Jeremy made this fix quickly, and it was not reviewed by anyone else. His management praised him for getting the job done with such dispatch.

Actually, "dys-patch" would have been a better description. Seven months later, a series of failures delayed the project for five weeks. It was eventually discovered that one of the intermediate modules in the calling tree had been changed so that it also modified the flag for condition X. Under these circumstances, WYA then re-modified the flag unbeknownst to the intermediate module, and created a logically inconsistent condition.

4.3.4. The ripple effect over time

Any programmer with more than a year's experience could cite at least a dozen "Jeremy stories." Notice how Jeremy's "solution" kept the ripple effect small early in the project, but leads to a very large ripple later. In a healthy project, the ripple effect should decrease over time, as indicated in Figure 4-9.

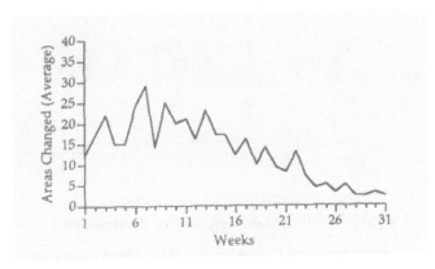

Figure 4-9. In a healthy project, the ripple effect should

107

decrease over time, because the changes with large scope should have been made early.

Figure 4-10 shows an unhealthy ripple effect curve. The two curves are from two projects within the same organization. Project 4-9 was close to budget and schedule. Project 4-10 was abandoned 11 months after its scheduled 6-month delivery, after running over budget by a factor of 2. Plotting the ripple effect at 6 months instead of in a post-mortem could have led to saving the project. Or, if management wasn't competent enough to save the project, they could have killed it at six months and save a great deal of money and aggravation.

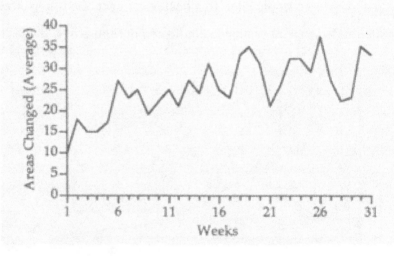

Figure 4-10. In an unhealthy project, the ripple effect can increase over time, showing that the scope of changes is increasing rather than decreasing as the project nears its

supposed completion date. This increase, or even lack of decrease, should serve as a warning to alert management.

4.3.5. The Titanic Effect

Figure 4-10 is a typical result of an accumulation of short-cuts that give an early appearance of speed. Perhaps the worst thing about these short-cuts is that they occur in an environment where management thinks that the code is "structured"—perhaps because it initially was well structured. The management of Project 4-10 believed they were protected against this sort of aberrant side-effect, so they relaxed their guard and thus were hit doubly hard in the fatal moment. I call this the "Titanic Effect."

The thought that disaster is impossible often leads to an unthinkable disaster.

"The rule in poker is that you don't lose your shirt on bad hands, but on hands that 'can't lose.' The owners of the Titanic 'knew' that their ship was unsinkable. They weren't going to waste time steering around icebergs, or wasted money having needless lifeboats."

Let there be no mistake. Left to itself, "structure" deteriorates. No matter how great your personal charm, or your luck, you're not going to get Nature to set aside the Second Law of Thermodynamics. Unless design integrity is explicitly controlled, such "short-cuts" cause the design integrity to deteriorate. If events are left to chance, the same phenomenon occurs with code quality and with documentation in all forms.

4.3.6. Maintaining maintainability

If maintainability is not explicitly maintained, a system becomes increasingly difficult to maintain as time goes on— another positive feedback loop. Figure 4-11 shows what this can lead to.

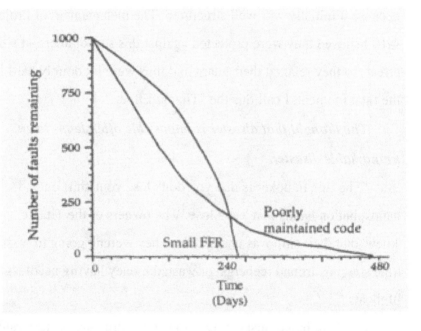

Figure 4-11. This is the result of a teaching simulation in which there are no faults created by fixing other faults, but the fixes are done in such a way as to reduce maintainability, so that later faults are harder to fix. As a result, the last faults seem to stay around longer than anticipated.

The figure shows the resolution of faults in two similar projects, one of which feeds back a certain number of faults (small FFR), but maintains maintainability. The other feeds back no faults (FFR = 0), but doesn't maintain maintainability. The result of the second project is a faster start, paid for with a long, drawn out tail as removing faults gets slower and slower. Of course, any real project will show a combination of the two effects, with their magnitude depending on the management control processes.

4.4 Helpful Hints and Suggestions

• As systems grow bigger, and as time delays grow longer, it becomes quite likely that a project will be simultaneously maintaining multiple versions of the same system. Multiple versions are tricky to handle even with the best of tools, and organizations in crisis seldom have adequate tools for maintaining their multiple versions. For an outsider, a quick look at the way versions are controlled will give a reliable prediction of the organization's pattern of software culture.

Multiple versions, of course, double and triple the burden of faults to be resolved, thus magnifying the basic resolution time. They also compound the difficulty of resolving each fault, because programmers may make changes without considering other changes that are being made simultaneously. Consequently, multiple versions cause the feedback ratio on side effects to be even greater, and increase the change of a "nuclear explosion."

• As a project proceeds, we will not usually know how many faults there are to be removed, so it will be impossible to plot graphs such as Figure 4-11. The rate of fault removal and STI resolution can be plotted, but these may give a false sense of what is happening. FFR and ripple effect, however, give a better idea of the state of the system. In addition, technical reviews can be used to give estimates of code quality and documentation currency.

• There is another essential component to maintainability: the competence of the crew, which is affected by turnover, training, and management attitude toward maintenance. Because people are naturally learners, the competence of the crew to maintain a particular system will tend to grow over time, possibly masking the deterioration of the code itself. But the crew's competence must also be maintained. largely by providing them tools, training, and resources for the job. If there should be a sudden exodus from the maintenance crew, management will suddenly discover how ugly a situation has been allowed to fester in the code, masked by the growing competence of the people.

4.5 Summary

1. Basic fault resolution dynamics are another case of Size/ Complexity Dynamics, with more faults and more complexity per fault leading to a non-linear increase in fault resolution time as

systems grow larger.

2. Side effects add more non-linearity to fault resolution. Either we take more time to consider side effects, or we create side effects when we change one thing and inadvertently change another.

3. The most obvious type of side effect is fault feedback, which can be measured by the Fault Feedback Ration (FFR). Fault feedback is the creation of faults while resolving other faults. Faults can be either functional or performance faults.

4. The FFR is a sensitive measure of project control breakdown. In a well-controlled project, FFR should decline as the project approaches its scheduled end.

5. One way to keep the FFR under control is to institute careful reviewing of fault resolutions, even if they are "only one line of code." The assumption that small changes can't cause trouble leads to small changes causing more trouble than bigger changes.

6. There are a number of ways in which a system deteriorates besides the addition of faults and performance inefficiencies, and these ways do not show up in ordinary project measurements. For instance, design integrity breaks down, documentation is not kept current, and coding style becomes patchy. All of these lead to a decrease in the system's maintainability.

7. When the integrity of a modular, or "black box," design

breaks down, the system shows a growing "ripple effect" from each change. That is, one change ripples through to cause many other changes.

8. If we are to avoid deterioration of systems, they must not only be maintained, but their maintainability must also be maintained.

9. Managers and developers often show overconfidence in the initial design as protection against maintenance difficulties. This kind of overconfidence can easily lead to a Titanic Effect, because the thought that nothing can go wrong with the code exposes the code to all sorts of ways of going wrong.

4.6. Practice

1. Draw a diagram of effects incorporating the evolution of the maintenance crew into the maintainability dynamic.

2. Tom DeMarco considers stories like the ripple effect on an operating system to be "fear tactics," and that people should be convinced of the proper software engineering practices without resorting to stories of people losing jobs and businesses going bankrupt. Discuss the tradeoff between telling the true outcome of such stories to make them harder to ignore and softening the stories to make them more palatable. If possible, draw a diagram of effects incorporating other factors in getting people to accept or reject new ideas.

3. Have you ever experienced a "Titanic" project? If so, prepare to discuss what might have been done to prevent a disaster. If not, why do you think you have not?

4. Estimate the ripple effect on a system with which you are involved. Do you think it is too high? What could be done to reduce it in one day? In a week? In a month? In a year?

5. What's the most bizarre side effect you can recall in your career in software? What's the most costly side effect? Get together a group of colleagues and share these side effect stories. See if you can extract any common elements found in bizarre and costly side effects.

Part V. Pressure Patterns

The great contribution of Pattern 2 to software engineering is the routinization of software development. As long as things go according to plan, Pattern 2 cultures can turn out valuable software at a reasonable price. But this great strength can become a weakness when things don't go according to plan. Routine managers may then behave in ways that turn a modest deviation into a full-fledged breakdown.

To readers who have worked in projects that have broken down, this Part of the volume may be the culmination of all our work to understand software thinking patterns. They have experienced managers who "manage by telling," and they have experienced managers who "manage a crisis by telling louder." They've always suspected there might be a better way, but perhaps have never had the good fortune to experience it. Once they have, I believe, they won't easily settle for "management by telling."

I would like to dedicate this Part to the memory of Bruce Oldfield, for something he said over 30 years ago. Bruce was one of the most competent software managers of his time, but like all of us, he had limits to how much pressure he could handle congruently. Here's the story:

The date of the first test flight for Project Mercury was rapidly approaching, and there were still three serious failures

116

unaccounted for in the tracking system. It was our goal in the project never to go into a flight with any serious failures unresolved, but the regular fault resolution procedures were getting nowhere with these three. At the weekly problem resolution meeting, I suggested that we form a special team of our best programmers to concentrate on these problems off-site. "A little clear thinking," I said, "is what we need."

The idea seemed to have considerable support from the other managers until Bruce stood up and looked me straight in the eye. I can still see him glowering at me, the THINK sign just over his head like a halo. "Listen," he said, "thinking is a luxury we can no longer afford!"

Over the years, I've heard the equivalent of that immortal phrase—so characteristic of Pattern 2 managers under pressure—dozens of times. Each time it makes me shudder, but also brings me back to the good old days in Project Mercury. There's something dramatic about working in a Routine organization that's falling apart under pressure, something you remember all your life. Still, there's enough drama of different kinds in Steering organizations, and we know we can produce quality software without abusing people. No, I won't have regrets if these chapters help managers improve their abilities, and ultimately eliminate the drama of the broken employee.

Chapter 5: Power, Pressure, and Performance

If you can keep your head when all about you

Are losing theirs and blaming it on you;

If you can trust yourself when all men doubt you,

But make allowance for their doubting too; ...

- "If," by Rudyard Kipling

Systems with non-linear dynamics are easily tipped into collapse. That's why we're so anxious about controlling them. Sometimes, however, the intended control mechanism actually contributes to the collapse. A crisis will rapidly occur in a controlled system when

1. The control actions are irrelevant, because they are at best linear attempts to counter a non-linear dynamic.

2. The control actions are backwards, in the sense that they actually contribute to making the dynamic non-linear, or more strongly non-linear.

In this chapter, we'll take a look at how Pattern 2 managers often respond to a potential crises by increasing the pressure they apply to workers, and how this pressure may indeed create the dynamic that triggers a breakdown. We'll also see some alternative management styles, such as used by Pattern 3 managers, that might offer a better way to stabilize performance.

5.1 The Pressure/Performance Relationship

In general, when human beings work in low pressure situations, their performance may be quite low. As most managers know, increasing the pressure may increase their performance—for a while. Thus, increasing pressure on the workers can be an effective control mechanism, if used correctly.

5.1.1 The linear model

Figure 5-1 shows the worst managers' understanding of the natural human dynamic in response to pressure. As one manager told me, "If you want performance, you look 'em in the eye and stare them down until you get commitment." Another expressed it this way, "More push; more production!"

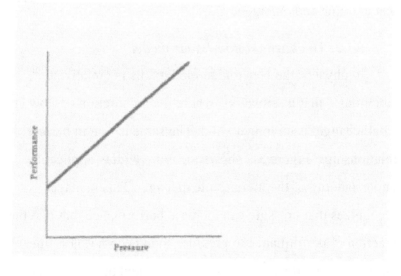

Figure 5-1. A poor manager's view of the natural human dynamic of pressure and performance is completely linear. The

119

more you push, the more you get.

This is the dynamic model in management that corresponds to Newton's model in physics:

Force = Mass x Acceleration

or

Acceleration = Force/Mass (Production = Push/ Resistance)

As in physics, this Newtonian model is a good approximate, linear model for many situations. When there is a fire in the theater or a mortar shell whistling toward the foxhole, there's no time for reasoned, fully participative discussion of every alternative course of action. I wonder, though, if software development ever needs that extreme and emergency.

5.1.2. The burnout non-linear model

In physics, the Newtonian model fails in "relativistic" situations—that is, situations where the assumption of slow speed, small change, is no longer valid. The same is true in human relationships. Figure 5-2 shows the more widely applicable understanding of the more astute manager. This manager recognizes that pressure can increase performance, but that the reaction of performance to pressure soon becomes non-linear. After a certain point, the curve slows its climb and then flattens out completely. This manager knows how to push people, but also knows how to take notice of signs that pushing is no longer leading to the same increment of performance.

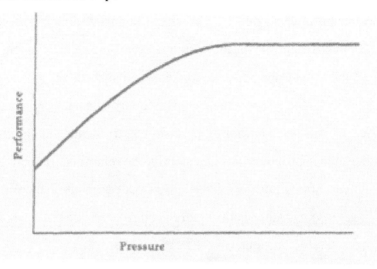

Figure 5-2. Increased pressure initially results in increased performance. Eventually, however, performance levels off as pressure continues to increase.

Managers call this flat part of the curve "burnout." People can recover from burnout, given rest, recreation, and time. Some managers actually recognize the burnout phenomenon, but simply view people as interchangeable parts. When one person-part burns out, you replace it with another one. This is what Curtis calls the "commodity view" of people. Perhaps the commodity view works in carrying sandbags, or in sausage factories, but in a software engineering project, when you lose a person, you lose a large part of the project.

5.1.3. The collapse non-linear model

But there is more to the pressure/performance relationship after burnout. Figure 5-3 shows our understanding of the general human dynamic over the whole range of pressure. This curve is found by psychologists in studies of all sorts of skilled performance under pressure—flying airplanes, taking examinations, assembling precision instruments, and, of course, computer programming. Evidently, the relationship is quite non-linear. Soon after the curve flattens out completely, the further response to additional pressure is an irreversible collapse, not a recoverable burnout.

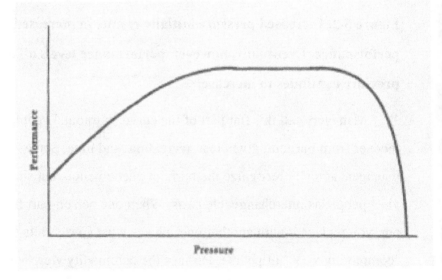

Figure 5-3. This is the general human response to pressure, found in all sorts of skilled performance, including programming. Increased pressure initially results in increased

performance. Eventually, performance levels off, then declines, then collapses as pressure continues to increase.

The flattening of the curve should be a warning to management to lower the pressure, but often is read as an indication to increase pressure even further. As the pressure increases beyond this point, performance starts to decrease, and then suddenly collapses. In a software project, you might see the collapse in a variety of forms—people quit, get sick, or go brain dead on the job. In each case, they no longer contribute to progress on the project, so their performance has gone to zero.

Actually, the worst situation occurs when they stay on the job and keep writing code. Pattern 2 managers might believe that their processes are so routinized that it doesn't matter if individual performance varies, and to a certain extent that is true. But no matter how routine your software process, it can't be done with zombies. They keep on writing code, all right—code with huge numbers of faults. In that case, we could justifiably say that performance has gone below zero. The longer these "living dead" are on the job, the worse the project's performance, no matter how routine the process.

5.2 Pressure To Find "The Last Fault"

Let's look in some detail at the consequences of the Pressure/ Performance Relationship in a common software engineering situation. Sometimes, when we get down to the job of locating the faults behind the last few STIs—as happens just before a release date—the location time dynamic is distorted by the application of management pressure (Figure 5-4).

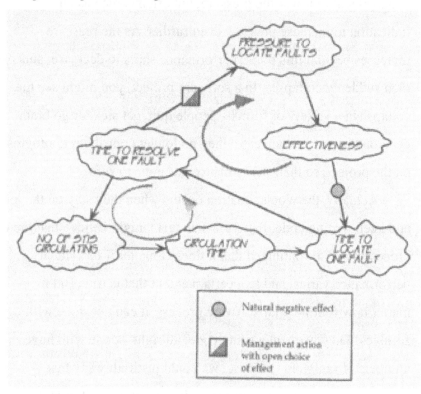

Figure 5-4. Increased pressure may result from desperation to resolve the last batch of STIs, especially as the time to find each fault gets longer and longer. Here we see this pressure added to a circulation dynamic to produce two potentially positive feedback loops indicated by the shaded arrows. Whether or not the top loop is positive depends on

**management's use of pressure in response to observed
performance in locating and resolving faults.**

As time goes by and significant STIs are still unresolved, the
pressure mounts. Sure enough, performance improves—for a
while. Then, without anyone realizing what's going on,
performance tapers off. The time to pin down the source of the
STIs becomes even longer, as illustrated by the teaching model
results in Figure 5-5.

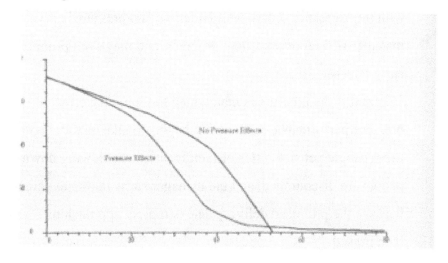

**Figure 5-5. Increased pressure on those attempting to locate
faults behind STIs leads to a faster initial rate of fault location.
If the pressure continues, however, the ultimate result may be a
much longer time to remove the final few STIs. In this model,
for example, there was still one STI remaining after 80 days,
whereas without added pressure, the last STI was resolved in**

53 days.

To understand this model, imagine that an enlightened manager, knowing the problems of size, selection, and circulation, decides to meet the planned release date by working the programmers under a small amount of extra pressure. A typical way to do this is to schedule paid overtime. For a while, this increased motivation does indeed lead to a more rapid location of STIs. Up until about week 40, things are looking very good indeed, with the "pressure" curve well under the "no pressure" curve. The manager will report excellent progress, and may even promise an early release.

But if the pressure is maintained too long, the effect of the pressure/performance relationship begins to take its toll. People are tired, people get sick, rates of fault location are slowing down so people are discouraged, and the manager starts railing at people because the promised delivery date is rapidly approaching—and then passed.

In the end, the entire fault location operation may collapse—which is one reason management often ships products with many known faults. In view of all the non-linear dynamics, this collapse should not surprise anyone, but it usually does.

5.3 Stress/Control Dynamic

Each individual has a unique pressure/performance curve,

though all the curves have the same general shape. Moreover, it's not the applied pressure that leads to the pressure/performance relationship, but the perceived pressure. What drives me to work 100 hours a week might simply provoke you to yawn.

Physicists make this distinction by calling the applied pressure "stress" and the reaction of the system, "strain." Unfortunately, the medical and psychological literature doesn't make this distinction, and neither do many managers. They use the term "stress" for both applied and perceived pressure, which tends to confuse their understanding of dynamics involving pressure. When you say, "I'm under a lot of stress," do you mean that a lot of pressure is being applied, or that you are reacting poorly to the pressure?

Once we make the distinction between the situation and the reaction to the situation, we can begin to investigate some details of different reactions to applied pressure. One set of psychological experiments demonstrates that the feeling of stress is tied into the feeling of control, by the dynamics illustrated in Figure 5-6 and Figure 5-7.

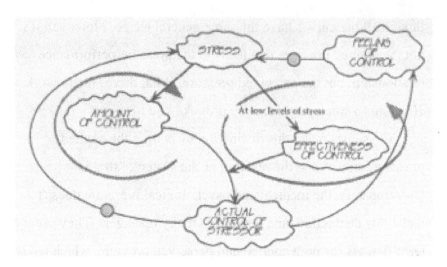

Figure 5-6. There are two major feedback loops involving stress and performance, because the relationship between stress and the ability to control is itself non-linear. Under low levels of felt stress, both feedback loops are stabilizing.

Figure 5-6 shows how stress is normally used, at low levels of stress. The stress you experience is information—a signal that things are getting a little out of control. You take some actions to get things back in control. If you are a competent controller, your actions are effective, so the more you act, the more you get the stressor under control. Your success is signaled by the reduction in felt stress. Examples would include:

Lack of sleep->headache->nap->sleep->reduced headache.

Work not finished->anxiety->working harder->work finished->good feeling.

Added to this loop is the loop on the right of the diagram, which indicates that stress is not only generated from the external stressor, but also by whether or not you feel in control of the situation. The feeling of being in control reduces stress, and the feeling of being out of control increases stress. Thus, your mental state influences, and is influenced by, your ability as a controller. If you know how to master your mental state, this gives you one more advantage in the struggle to be an effective controller. To the extent that your mental state is out of your control, your presence might be the very factor that sends the situation into the collapse dynamic of Figure 5-7.

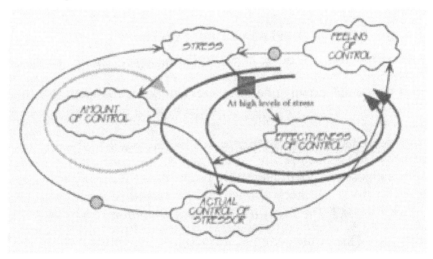

Figure 5-7. Under high levels of felt stress, the right-hand feedback loops become de-stabilizing, which explains the breakdown of performance.

In Figure 5-7 we see that the only thing changed from the diagram Figure 5-6 is the influence of the arrow from stress to effectiveness of control. This represents the downward portion of the stress/performance curve. Once this has happened, you—the supposed controller—begin to act ineffectively. At the same time, the number of control actions increases, so you are being ineffective more often. This contributes to the worsening of the situation, and also makes you feel even more out of control, both of which increase your felt stress. These two cooperating cycles create a sure-fire recipe for breakdown. The only question is who will break down first, you or the system you're trying to control.

5.4 Forms of Breakdown Under Pressure

Organizations and individuals also differ in the details of how they break down under pressure. Our particular interest is in the breakdown in controllers. Let's look at a few of the more common breakdown dynamics seen in the Pattern 2 mechanisms that are supposed to control software projects.

5.4.1 The Pressure/Judgment Dynamic

One of the common ways to lose your effectiveness as a controller is to lose your ability to observe accurately. For instance, you may succumb to the social pressures from others in the project who want you to see things through their rose-colored glasses.

Once your judgment starts to go, you lock yourself into this version of a pressure/performance breakdown:

pressure ->conformity ->misestimating ->lack of control ->more pressure

Once this cycle starts, managers will find it impossible to get the kind of information they need to exercise control over a project. The typical interaction goes like this:

Manager: "How's it going?"

Worker: "Nothing I can't handle."

Manager: "Great. Keep up the good work."

Understanding this dynamic allows the Steering manager to beat this effect by decoupling the flow of information from the pressure cycle. One way to do this is by having measurements that are taken automatically, without human intervention. Another way is to take secret surveys, so that nobody knows whose response said that there is zero probability that the project will be finished on time.

5.4.2 The Lost Labor Dynamic

Another way Pattern 2 controllers often break down is by losing the ability to act, or at least to act quickly and effectively. Brooks's Law tells us how adding workers late in a project slows down the project. One wag suggested that if Brooks's Law is true, then the way to get projects done on time is to subtract workers at a late date. Unfortunately, subtraction doesn't work that way, and is, in fact, even worse than adding.

Figure 5-8 shows one part of the dynamic of losing experienced workers late in a project. Each time a worker is lost, the amount of raw labor is obviously reduced. At the same time, there is additional coordination work to sort out the lost person's tasks. These two effects, however, don't create a feedback loop, but since they slow down the project, management may step up the pressure on the remaining workers. Or, they may step up the pressure on themselves. In either case, the increased pressure may lead to more people leaving (either physically or mentally), and now the loop is complete.

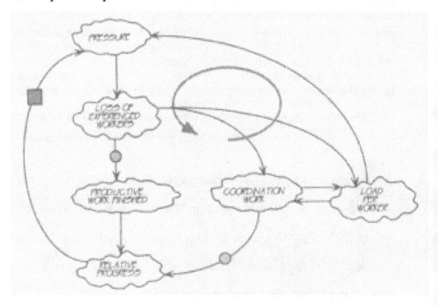

Figure 5-8. Losing workers late in a project increases the pressure on the remaining workers, which makes it likely that

they, too, will be lost to the project.

5.4.3 The Pile-On Dynamic

Losing workers is one thing. A worse thing is when the controllers start acting in destructive ways in response to stress. A curious feedback loop can be set in motion by management at any time the software workload is increased, as indicated in Figure 5-9. When managers have more work to be assigned, the first place they tend to look is to the people who have the most knowledge of the system. The people who get all the assignments, of course, are the people who get the most chance to acquire more knowledge of the system, so they are the ones who are most likely to be chosen the next time there is additional work to do.

This loop creates a lock-on of knowledge, because whomever gets the first few assignments becomes the expert, to the exclusion of the others. But the other side of this lock-on of knowledge is the "pile-on" of work to be done, which often leads to burnout or collapse of the most critical people in a project.

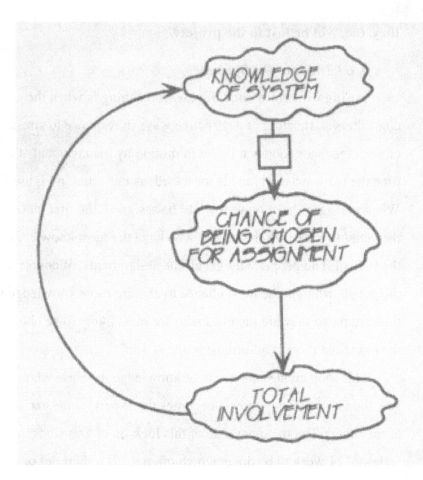

Figure 5-9. It's only natural to pile work onto your best people, which also naturally leads to overload, burnout, and breakdown.

Steering managers who want to avoid the loss of their most critical people learn to recognize their own involvement in this "pile-on dynamic," and take control of their own actions, as shown in Figure 5-10. Managers have two control points in this diagram:

1. They can choose less knowledgeable people, for the training value.

2. They can choose those people with the least work to do.

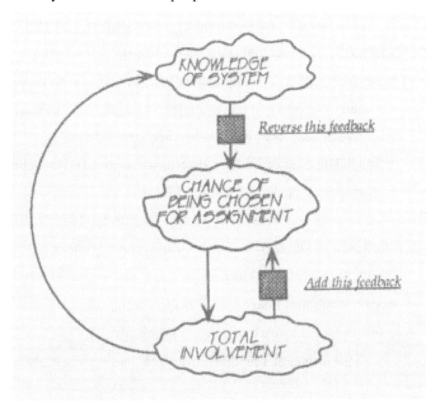

Figure 5-10. Piling on can be stopped by reversing natural unconscious tendencies.

Each of these interventions has a problem, of course. The first must be started early, not when the crunch has already arrived. The second may be seen as rewarding the least competent people. But perhaps the people with the least work to do are those that truly know the most about the system—for they are the ones who are most in control of their situation.

5.4.4 The Panic Reaction

Another way that controllers become ineffective under pressure is by going into panic. In panic, their actions are not simply ineffective or counter-effective. They either freeze and can't act at all or go into a frenzy of irrelevant action. Once management goes into a panic, the project is doomed unless the panic is immediately arrested or the managers are removed—which may trigger another panic in someone else.

Panic is a well-defined physiological state, whose dynamic is illustrated in Figure 5-11. The cycle can start anywhere, but often begins with an external physical or emotional trigger. In Routine software cultures, I have seen managers going into a physiological panic triggered by each of non-routine events:

• the arrival of a report showing that one module has slipped a week

• a programmer asking for two days off to get married

• the announcement of a visit from upper management

• a team leader reporting that two team members would be going to a class

• the arrival of a consultant

136

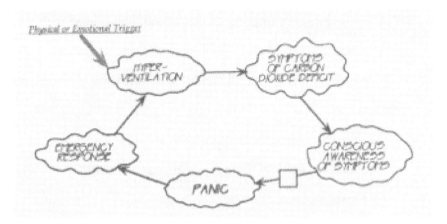

Figure 5-11. Panic is a positive feedback phenomenon, based on a cycle of physical and mental reactions to some external trigger.

The trigger, however, cannot be said to cause the panic. The cause of the panic is the way your personal system is set up. In response to the trigger, you start to hyperventilate. This instantaneous reaction can't be avoided because it's built into your body. If hyperventilation continues for a few moments, it leads to carbon dioxide deficit in the blood, which leads to some of the following symptoms:

- uncomfortable awareness of the heart (palpitations)
- racing heart (tachycardia)
- heartburn, chest pain
- dizziness and lightheadedness, poor concentration
- blurred vision

137

• numbness or tingling of the mouth, hands, and feet

• shortness of breath, "asthma," choking sensation

• lump in the throat, difficulty in swallowing, stomach pain, nausea

• muscle pains, shaking, muscle spasms

• tension, anxiety, fatigue, weakness, sweating

• poor sleep, nightmares

As you become aware of one or more of these symptoms, you start giving yourself messages interpreting the symptoms, because once again, it's not the event that counts, but your reaction to the event. Normally, you might interpret these symptoms in a relatively benign way, such as, "Oh, I'm really overtired and stressed out." But in a panic-prone individual, the interpretation becomes, "Oh my God! Something awful is going to happen!" In that case, the feeling of emergency leads to further hyperventilation, and the cycle goes around once more.

We all go into panic some of the time, but normal people quickly recover when they become aware that their life is not threatened if someone takes off two days to get married. People who cannot easily recover from their instant panic reactions should not be in project work, let alone in project management. Unfortunately, they may be attracted to Pattern 2 project management, because of its promise to eliminate all surprised through the total routinization of work. Instead of trying to control everyone else as a way of dealing with their inability to control themselves, they should be getting professional help—which has a good chance of being successful.

5.5 Management of Pressure

Some managers don't just overload people in response to stress. Acting as if they are in continual panic, they overload their projects as a matter of principle. Figure 5-12 shows the basic dynamic of the chronically overloaded project.

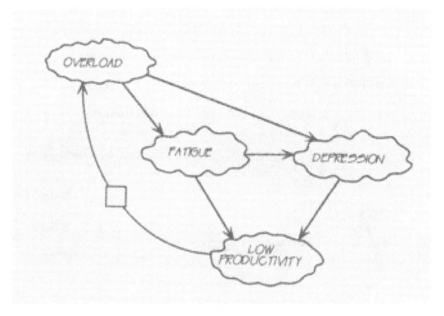

Figure 5-12. Chronic overload is self-perpetuating. Conversely, reducing the load early in a project can have a positive snowball effect.

5.5.1. The self-regulating worker

The manager's idea in chronically overloading a project is to take advantage of the linear part of the pressure/performance curve —to keep everyone operating at their "top efficiency." This is the direct effect from overload to low productivity. At the same time, chronic overload risks wearing people out and turning their morale towards depression, both of which tend to reduce productivity.

Figure 5-13 shows the dynamic of an organization that responds well to this kind of overload strategy. This organization is characterized by self-regulated workers, individuals who carry the best of Pattern 1 culture. When they become fatigued, they recognize their fatigue and take whatever steps they need to reduce their fatigue. When their morale droops, they recognize the droop and take whatever steps they need to raise their morale.

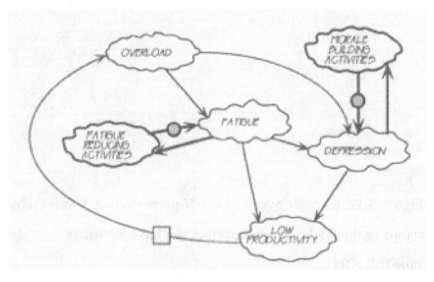

Figure 5-13. This is the overload dynamic of an organization characterized by self-regulated workers, who know how to take care of themselves in the face of overload.

5.5.2. The disempowering manager

For chronic overload to work as a tactic, however, it's not sufficient for the workers to be self-regulating. In addition, their managers must be empowering. That is, they must trust the workers enough to let them regulate themselves as they see fit. Unfortunately, I've encountered very few Routine managers of the overload persuasion who also believe in empowerment. Instead, their reaction to their workers' attempts to self-regulate are to block all possible avenues of stress reduction.

Whether the overall result of continuous management pressure is positive is a matter of balance among these effects. Pattern 2 projects often stay in balance until they come close to some scheduled delivery date, at which point overload reactions cut in and destroy the balance. At that point, the typical management response is to

- cancel all vacations for the duration
- mandate scheduled overtime
- prohibit compensatory time off for overtime worked
- void all travel plans
- cancel all course enrollments

• put all applications for sick leave under microscopic scrutiny

• eliminate all "frivolity," such as office parties and sporting events

• monitor the cafeterias for "excessive" lunch breaks

• break up all hallway conversation

In short, they do their utmost to get rid of any activity that might reduce fatigue or raise morale. To compensate, they may begin to issue memos urging the workers to greater efforts in service of the Great Cause. Anyone with any project experience at all knows how effective these memos are. Pattern 3 managers know that they are effective — as indications of impending breakdown.

5.5.3. The Law of Diminishing Response

The Pressure/Performance curve of Figure 5-3 sometimes goes up and sometimes goes down. To represent this U-shape in a diagram of effects, we need put in extra boxes or extra lines, which can make the diagram hard to read. However, instead of plotting the height of the performance curve, we can plot its slope, as in Figure 5-14. That is, instead of measuring performance versus pressure, we measure how responsive performance is to added pressure at various levels.

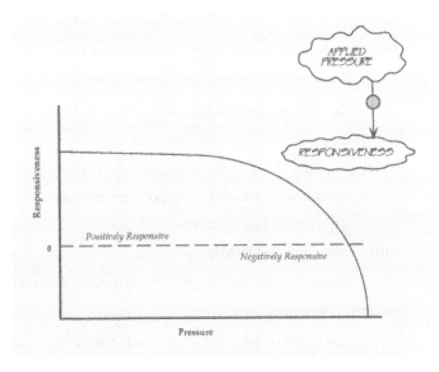

Figure 5-14. Although performance actually moves in different directions in response to pressure, the slope of the performance always moves in the same direction—downward. We can reasonably call this slope "responsiveness." Responsiveness always decreases as management pressure increases, although for a while it will be relatively flat before it starts to plunge.

Responsiveness, defined this way, is always a decreasing function of increased pressure. This allows us to represent the relationship between responsiveness and pressure with the simple diagram of effects shown alongside the graph. This diagram says,

143

succinctly, that the greater the applied pressure, the less people respond to it. In effect, it is a Law of Diminishing Response:

The more pressure you add, the less you get for it.

5.5.4. The responsive manager

Putting all of these dynamics together, we begin to see how a Steering manager thinks. A Unlike the Routine manager, the Steering manager can successfully apply management pressure as a control intervention. To get maximum productivity out of workers, such a manager must do two things:

1. Allow—and encourage—workers to regulate their own response to pressure.

2. Use responsiveness, rather than performance, as the clue to applying pressure.

Figure 5-15 shows how a Steering manager uses the Law of Diminishing Response as a guide to successful control interventions. When you consider adding some pressure, the key variable to monitor is not a person's performance, but their responsiveness. How are they responding to the existing pressures? When they hear a new "challenge," do they drop their head a quarter of an inch and mumble an acceptance under their breath? Do they become annoyed and give a hundred reasons why it can't be done? Do they show external signs of panic? These are all signs that they've reached the point where responsiveness has gone

144

negative, yet they are unable to control their own response.

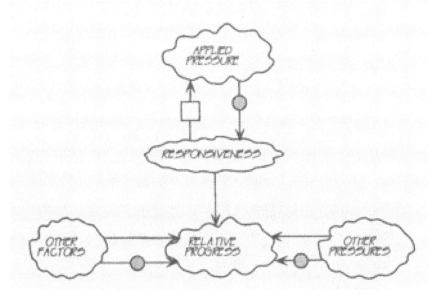

Figure 5-15. The competent manager recognizes that there are other pressures on a person and other factors influencing performance, and so regulates applied management pressure based on observed responsiveness, not on performance.

Or are they alert and genuinely enthusiastic, able to ask penetrating questions that need answering before accepting the extra work? Can they consciously trade off less important work for high priority assignments? These are signs that their responsiveness is still above zero, so it's okay to pile a little more fuel on the fire—but not make any assumptions about next time.

Once you're able to be responsive to other people's responsiveness, then you can turn the same approach on yourself.

What is your reaction when you get added pressure from your own manager, or from your customers? Do you drop your head and mumble? Do you give a hundred reasons why not? Do you panic? If so, what are you doing to regulate your own morale and fatigue?

Figure 5-16 shows a modification of the teaching simulation in Figure 5-5, with the pressure applied by management in relation to responsiveness, rather than performance. Time to clear all STIs has been reduced from 53 days with no pressure to 48 days with intelligently added pressure. It shows that, at least in theory, responsive management can actually speed up an "unmanageable" process such as testing. Just think what it could do with more manageable processes!

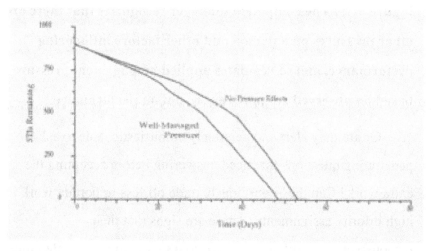

Figure 5-16. A revision of the simulation in Figure 5-5 shows that the responsive manager may be able to speed up the testing process by adjusting pressure according to

responsiveness.

5.6 Helpful Hints and Suggestions

• It's hard to see, in yourself, the external signs of being over-pressured. One way to monitor yourself is to note that pressure works through the Size/Complexity Dynamic. Pressure adds one or more new factors for you to control, which makes your job of exercising control just that much more complex. So, you can tell whether you're under too much pressure by noticing how many messages you're giving yourself that are trying to reduce the complexity of the situation—especially if they are "magical" solutions that take care of everything at once. Examples might include,

• "I'm trying to keep my manager from firing me."

• "I'm looking for another job."

• "I'm preparing my resume."

• "If only I had time to find someone to wash my clothes."

• People respond to pressure differently, and we don't know many of the reasons. One reason we do know about is age. Older workers are more skilled, so they generally know better how to handle additional pressure. They've seen it before. On the other hand, older workers tend to have more outside pressures, such as, family concerns and issues about their own health.

One dynamic that we know for sure is that every day,

everyone gets a day older. Often, startup organizations experience a "growing older" dynamic. At the beginning, their typical programmer is 22 years old, lean and hungry, unmarried, with no previous job experience, and in good health. After ten years of success, their average programmer is 32 years old, 15 pounds heavier, married (and possibly divorced) with 1.7 children, 25 years of job experience (crammed into 10 years of real time), and rather tired out. Most important, they must be managed differently, because don't respond to pressure in the same way they did 10 years ago.

• Even when managers don't add to the pressure, it tends to mount as schedule dates grow near. Managers often try to relieve this pressure by taking late steps, but they rarely relieve this pressure, and often add to it. Examples of this kind of intervention include:

• Brooks's Law: adding people late to help relieve the workload

• making small slips in the schedule, which often backfires

• unconsciously communicating a feeling of disappointment and disgrace

• adding interesting functions at last minute to "motivate" the workers

• holding official "pep rallies" to build morale

The best intervention is to start the project right, manage it right, and then let it do it's thing, approaching its scheduled dates in a natural manner—for better or worse. If you haven't done it right for two years, what makes you think you can now do the right thing to correct it all in two weeks?

5.7 Summary

1. The Pressure/Performance Relationship says that added pressure can boost performance for a while, then starts to get no response, then leads to collapse.

2. Pressure to find the last fault can easily prolong the time to find the last fault, perhaps indefinitely.

3. The Stress/Control Dynamic explains that we not only respond to the external pressures, but to internal pressures we place on ourselves when we think we are losing control. This dynamic makes the Pressure/Performance Relationship even more non-linear.

4. Breakdown under pressure comes in many forms. Judgment may be the first thing to go, especially in response to peer pressure to see things their way.

5. As people leave a project, either physically or mentally, it adds pressures to the remaining people, who are then more likely to leave themselves.

6. Managers may create a Pile-On Dynamic by choosing to

give new assignments only to those people who are already the reigning experts. This adds to their load, and their expertise, which makes it more likely they'll get the next assignment.

7. Some people respond to stress with a Panic Reaction, even though the situation is not anything like life-threatening. Such people must not be in high-stress projects, or they will only add to the stress.

8. Pressure can be managed. It helps if the workers are self-regulating, the managers are empowering, and that responsiveness, rather than performance, is used to measure readiness for more pressure.

5.8. Practice

1. Draw a diagram of effects for the relationship between applied pressure and professional development on the the part of the technical staff. Include effects of explicit training, implicit training through group work, and the effects of turnover on average experience level. What are the implications of your diagram for the improvement of a development organization over time?

2. Draw a diagram of effects on the relationship between the age structure of a population of developers and their performance on projects.

3. Remember a time when you panicked. What messages did

you give yourself? Write down these messages and get a group of colleagues to share their messages. For each message, what countermessage could you use? If you don't know, one of your colleagues has probably solve the problem already. Why do you think this is so?

4. Have you ever been a victim of the pile-on dynamic? What did you do to extricate yourself? What would you do next time to prevent it happening in the first place?

5. Have you ever stood on the sidelines while someone else got all the good assignments piled on? What would you do the next time to ensure that you got your share?

6. What's your characteristic reaction to burnout? What would you like your manager to do when this symptom becomes evident? What prevents you from telling your manager that before you burn out the next time? What prevents you from asking your own employees what you should watch for in them, and what they'd like you to do?

Chapter 6: Handling Breakdown Pressure

"Time wounds all heels." - Anonymous

Poorly managed pressure can lead to collapse, but it's not always clear *where* the system will actually break down. In software projects, time pressure is almost universal, and "time wounds all heels." Time pressure finds the Achilles Heel of any culture. In Pattern 2 cultures, what usually collapses first under time pressure is the manager's ability to make meaningful control interventions.

6.1 Shuffling Work

One characteristic behavior of an over-pressured manager is to shuffle work around in ritualistic ways, hoping that rearrangement will accomplish get something for nothing. This behavior is a caricature of a management behavior that could sometimes be meaningful, if exercised when things had not already begun to collapse.

6.1.1 Task splitting

During a time crisis, most people are juggling many tasks at one time. In fact, one symptom of overload is the number of people assigned 1/2 time to project A, 1/7 time to project B, 1/23 time to project C, and so forth. Tasks keep coming up, and management simply adds tasks to existing staff, perhaps because they've heard of Brooks's Law and don't want to add staff late in the project.

Task splitting, however, has a dynamic very much like Brooks's Law, as seen in Figure 6-1. As with Brooks's Law, the new tasks add learning time to the already overloaded staff. Deciding among these tasks adds coordination time, and now there is the additional loss each time we switch from one task to another. Any person assigned to more than three tasks will lose at least half of their time to switching. Pattern 2 management seems to forget this fundamental rule when the crisis starts to push. Instead, they start to see not human beings, but boxes on process charts. With automated tools, it's easy to put one name in two boxes, so what's the problem?

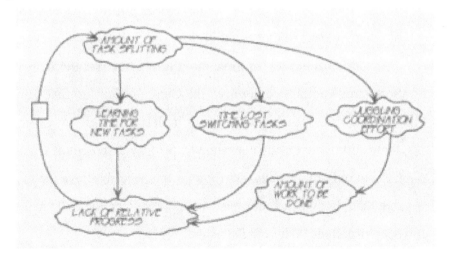

Figure 6-1. One way to attempt to beat Brooks's Law is to avoid adding people by giving new tasks to experienced people. Task splitting, however, has its own dynamic, which actually

leads to the same effect as Brooks's Law—slowing down the project.

About the only factor that prevents this tactic from having worse results is that most overloaded people assigned a new task simply ignore it. Or ignore the old one. Or both. The only one who gets an extra load is the managers, who spend time shuffling "assignments" around on their project management software.

6.1.2 Everything is Number One Priority

Ignoring new tasks is a way of assigning priority, because any time there are many tasks to perform, they must be done in some priority order. Often during a crisis, the only directive from management is "*everything* is number one priority." Here's a story of what happens in that situation:

After struggling for three months at Select Southern Software, we finally convinced the General Manager that slow response time was the major factor in delaying their key project. At some additional cost, we arranged a priority shipment of a new CPU in only two weeks. We thought this would relieve the overload, but when I returned two months later, the CPU had not been installed. "Why not?" I asked.

"We're waiting for a cable," was the General Manager's reply.

"But you have your own cable shop, downstairs?"

"Yes, but they told us they had higher priority work to do."

"But this is your *highest* priority."

"Yes, we told them, but they didn't do it."

I walked with the General Manager down to the cable shop. We found that they were holding up the CPU cable because of another order that the office manager had told them was "Number One Priority." We introduced the General Manager, whom nobody in the cable shop had ever met. Then we all stood there for 25 minutes chatting while the shop workers made the CPU cable.

Many priority systems are ineffective because "everything is number one priority." The way this comes about is easy to understand by looking at the Priority Dynamic shown in Figure 6-2. This sort of system may work if there's not much pressure, but if there's not much pressure, why do you have a priority system?

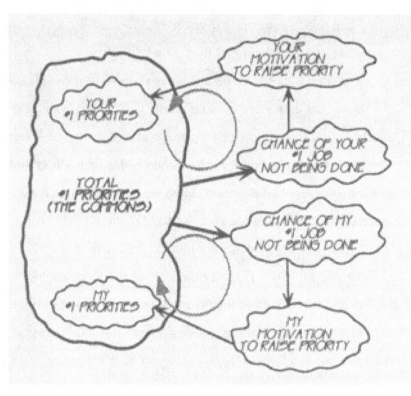

Figure 6-2. If there is no restraint on the allocation of priority, then all priorities tend to move to the highest level, each driven by a positive feedback loop. This is a phenomenon well known in ecology as The Tragedy of the Commons, which explains why common lands tend to be overgrazed or deforested.

If a priority system is to work at all, there must be some sort of negative feedback control to spread out the priority assignments among the different rankings. This should be the job of a manager who receives information about competing priorities and who sits at a level high enough to resolve conflicts for the greater good. Of course, this manager must also be able to act congruently under time pressure, not the manager who hides in the office and shuffles assignments.

Money is an excellent way to keep the "commons" from being overused, but any limited resource can be used in the same way. You tie the limited resource to the priority system so that each person has a fixed amount of "priority" to use. If the resource is truly limited, this breaks their feedback loop, or at least stabilizes it short of "everything is first priority."

6.1.3 Choosing your own priority

"Everything is number one priority" is actually equivalent to setting *no* priority, another common management practice in Pattern 2. In the absence of clear directives on what must be done first, people are free to make their own choices. Since they are generally unaware of the overall goals of the organization, they tend to suboptimize, choosing whatever looks good to them at the moment.

In one organization, I interviewed a number of programmers who were handling STIs. When asked why she had chosen a particular task, one programmer explained, "This customer is an SOB. If I solve this problem, he'll stop calling me."

Another programmer in the same organization said, "I'm solving this problem because the customer is so nice to me. The ones who get abusive on the phone go to the bottom of my stack.

157

Besides, he has to call long distance."

A third programmer explained, "I do the customer work last. The jobs I have to do for the development staff come first, partly because it's more important work, but mostly because they're right across the hall."

In three interviews, I had identified the following "priority" rules:

- SOBs get highest priority.
- SOBs get lowest priority.
- Whoever's farthest gets highest priority.
- Whoever's closest gets highest priority.
- Whichever work I decide is most important gets highest priority.

The result of this type of "prioritizing" is a more or less random order to the way the jobs get done—typical of the ineffectiveness of a Routine organization trying to handle exceptions.

6.1.4 Doing the easiest task first

Believe it or not, there are actually worse control tactics than a random priority scheme. In order to get some feeling of accomplishment, when people have a choice of tasks to do, they often choose the *easiest* task first, so as to "do something." This decision process gives a short-term feeling of relief, but in the long term results in an accumulation of harder and harder problems.

As we saw earlier, all faults are not created equal. The Failure Detection Curve showed that the last fault located is more difficult to locate than the first, and that's only *unconscious* selection. When the organization is feeling the pressure of a crisis, we can add to this effect the *conscious* selection processes whereby people set aside or avoid any problem they think will be difficult.

When we simulate the time to clean up all faults in a system, we must add a component that takes this distortion into account. Figure 6-3 shows the results of a teaching simulation showing how this selection effect could increase the time to locate the source of the last STI in our 90,000 line system. One curve shows how the STIs would be located if all STIs were treated equally. The other shows what happens with a selection effect added—easy STIs being handled before hard ones are tackled. And, of course, effect will be even worse if we add the time to *resolve* the faults to the simulation.

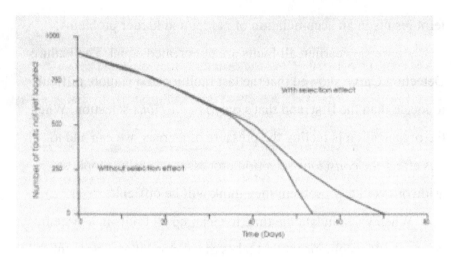

Figure 6-3. We first locate those problems that are easiest to locate, thus leaving the more difficult ones for the end. This Selection Effect lengthens the time to locate the final failure. Early estimates based on the rate of location cannot distinguish between these two curves.

Notice how the time is extended from 53 to 72 working days, though even at the 25-day mark the difference between the two curves is essentially non-detectable. Thus management has no warning—unless they understand the "worst-last" selection process.

Sometimes management installs a system of rewarding developers for the *number* of customer problems solved. Clearly, this encourages programmers to tackle the easiest ones first, and under crisis conditions, management is unaware of what they have induced. Thus, their progress estimates are always optimistic.

160

We find a similar tendency to optimism in the testing department. Some tests are harder to administer than others. Some tests cannot be administered until the blocking faults detected by other tests are cleared away. Tackling the easiest tests first leaves all the hardest tests for the last. If test "progress" is being reported to management by "number of tests completed," then when 80% of the tests have been done, perhaps 95% of the testing *effort* is still ahead.

6.1.5 Circulating hot potatoes

Another way an individual can relieve overload is by passing problems to other people. As a result, in a quality crisis, problems don't get solved, they merely circulate. We've already seen this problem with handling of STIs.

In one client, the company average remaining STI had been circulating for 7.5 months. We found one that had been circulating for almost three years. Some of this circulation was simply poor administration, but most was caused by the practice of moving STIs to another desk in order to show "progress" on management reports.

Problem circulation is usually the result of an spasmodic management style that punishes people who happen to be holding a problem when the manager's interest reawakens. This dynamic is exactly equivalent to the children's game of "hot potato," so we don't need to simulate it. All you need to do is give some seven-year-olds a potato and watch what happens. Under hot potato management, of course, it's not only STIs that circulate. Any problem that doesn't have an immediate, obvious solution will show this same dynamic if management punishes the person who happens to be holding it when the bell rings.

6.2 Ways of Doing Nothing

Passing problems around quickly is an effective way of doing nothing, but there are many more effective ways of doing nothing. Observing how many people are in fact doing nothing is a good way to assess the load on a project, so let's look at a few of the most common techniques.

6.2.1 Accepting poor quality products

The first clear fact available to demonstrate overload is the poor quality of the products being developed. When measurements are made of the quality of work in progress, managers have early warnings of the crisis. Unfortunately, Pattern 2 organizations that experience quality crises seldom have reliable systems of quality measurements. And, if they do have such a system, it's the first thing to be sacrificed when the pressure mounts.

The lack of measurement defends poor management. It's easier to deny the existence of poor quality when no measurements are made of the quality of work in progress. Eventually, however, products are delivered to customers. Once the product is in customer hands, it becomes more difficult to deny poor quality—but not impossible.

Pattern 2 cultures are usually rather adept at denying the existence of poor quality. One hardware company actually gave a $50,000 award to the team that developed a compiler because there was only one STI in the first year after shipment. When we investigated that STI, we found that it was a fault that made it impossible to install the compiler in the operating system. Thus, the reason there were no STIs was that the compiler was of such poor quality that nobody was using it!

The only truly reliable way to find out about the quality of your shipped products is to speak directly to the people who are using them—not their purchasing department, nor their managers, but the actual users. Even there, it is possible for people trapped in a crisis mentality to deny poor quality.

After a devastating user group meeting, one manager told me, "Look, only the chronic complainers show up at these user meetings. The satisfied users are home using our system." In a few months, he was home, too, drawing unemployment compensation.

6.2.2 Not accepting schedule slippage

When there is no reliable direct measurement of product quality, it's still possible for the dedicated investigator to read some less direct signs. One thing we always look for is schedule slippage, which we've seen is always a euphemism for poor quality.

In a well-managed project, schedule slippage on some component of the system *may* mean only moderately poor quality. When acceptance tests are not all satisfied, the component is held back. When this happens, it's a good idea for the manager to find out exactly which tests were not passed, and perhaps get an independent appraisal of how serious they are. The testers and developers themselves are always a bit too optimistic for a reliable picture.

In poorly managed projects, there may not even *be* any explicit, pre-determined acceptance tests for components. In that case, we can predict that quality will *always* be poor, but schedule slippage indicates *outrageously* poor quality. Why? Because without explicit tests, component functionality testing is simply run forward into systems testing. Developers will pass the component on to the next stage when it merely compiles clean and runs to end of job without crashing something. Therefore, if they can't even get *that* far, you can be 99% sure that the overall component quality stinks.

In poorly managed projects, of course, "making the schedule" doesn't imply quality. There won't even be meaningful component delivery schedules, so the only time you become aware of slippage is when the entire product is due to be shipped. And when somebody points out to management that the system doesn't work, management says, "We'll ship it to the customer and call it maintenance." A manager who *cannot* slip a schedule has no standard of quality—and thus is actually doing nothing.

6.2.3 Accepting resource overruns

Of course, there's always *some* standard of quality, if only in the hearts and minds of the developers. Any programmer, no matter how inept, has some reservations about releasing total junk. Thus, if the developers feel that their component isn't ready, they will try to hold it back.

Some managers, however, don't understand Brooks's Law. They will meet any request for schedule slippage with promises of extra resources—because "the schedule is not negotiable." With such a management style, extra resources become a reliable sign of poor quality, and you can be sure that the organization will feel the full non-linear dynamic of Brook's Law.

Terrible managers, of course, will meet a request for schedule slippage not with promises, but with threats. In that case, resources will not increase, and the schedule will be "met." Consequently, if management is terrible enough, we can't make any inferences about quality from being on time and under budget. This is Weinberg's Zeroth Law of Software:

If the software doesn't have to work, you can always meet any other requirement.

6.2.4 Managers not available

One kind of resource consumption can always be used as a reliable indicator of an impending quality crisis. When managers are overloaded, then we know that the control system is overloaded. Why does a control system overload? As Figure 6-4 shows, the amount of controller activity is itself controlled by the amount of uncontrolled system behavior. When the system shows signs of going out of bounds, the controller swings into action. If that action is effective, the system's uncontrolled behavior will diminish, and therefore the controller's activities will also diminish.

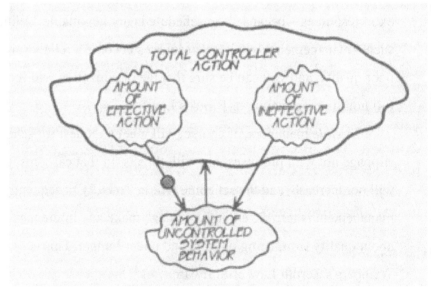

Figure 6-4. An effective controller will be busy from time to time, but a controller that is *always* busy is by definition

ineffective.

In other words, we are not speaking of short-term overloads. A crunch lasting a week or two will occur in any normal project. Longer crunches will not occur, however, because an effective control system will bring them quickly to an end. Therefore, when managers are out of touch for longer than a week or two, it must be that their attempted control interventions aren't working, or are working backwards.

Managers often say that it's not their fault that they're so busy, and they are often right. Outside factors may indeed be too disturbing to be regulated, but that's usually because managers at a higher level are not doing an effective job of regulating the outside factors. When upper levels of management pass down the pressure, the project is subject to the dynamic shown in Figure 6-5. In household terms, this dynamic is equivalent to holding a blowtorch on a thermostat in an attempt to warm the room.

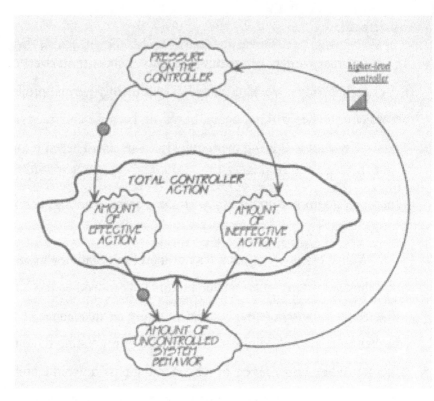

Figure 6-5. Higher levels of control can interfere with lower levels by putting pressure on the lower controllers past the point of improved performance. The lower controller's ineffective action then amplifies the amount of uncontrolled behavior.

This kind of higher level ineptness does tend to make it impossible for a lower level controller to be effective. Whatever the originating level, however, the conclusion is the same: at some level the managers are not acting effectively, or,

Busy managers mean bad management.

168

Managers who lack self-confidence, of course, will always *say* they are busy. It isn't befitting a Pattern 2 manager to admit to slack time. You can test the quality of management by interviewing employees and finding out how long they had to wait to see their manager for an unscheduled contact. Also notice how many employees tell you they no longer bother trying to see their manager without a long-standing appointment.

Some of these employees use E-mail, and with some E-mail systems we can also tabulate the response time for a brief response. If the drop-in time or E-mail response time remains greater than 24 hours for a couple of weeks, a crisis is well on its way.

These tests for management slack do not mean I advocate "management by reaction." On the contrary, I advocate "management by proaction." To be proactive, however, a manager must have time to

- gather information outside of normal channels
- digest information from the normal channels
- consider a variety of alternatives
- sell a plan of action
- adjust plans in the face of day-to-day realities.

Thus, if managers don't have a reserve of time, they *cannot* be managing effectively. In a well-run project, nowhere near a crisis, the managers may put in a full day, but they have lots of time to damp out crises before they get off the ground.

6.2.5 No time to do it right

"We don't have time to do it right" seems to be the motto of the organization in crisis.

In one startup software company, I saw this sign in the president's office:

Why is it we never have time to do it right but we always have time to do it over?

Unfortunately, his sign proved to be overly optimistic. They kept doing things wrong, and before they had time to do them over, they went bankrupt.

In effect, this president was saying that he knew the right way to develop software, and that the way they were working was wrong, but that he couldn't do anything about it. It's bad enough not to know what you're doing, but it's far worse to know and then take shortcuts. It's even worse if you're supposed to be the leader of the organization, to whom everyone looks for guidance. The president sets the tone for the culture, but usually does it unconsciously. That's why Crosby insists, and I agree, that quality improvement must begin at the top. The president is always holding a control like that of Figure 6-5—a control that can undermine all controls lower down in the organization.

6.3 Short-Circuiting Procedures

When schedule is all-important, and people are overloaded,

everybody is desperately seeking relief. If the crisis is short-term, one useful tactic that may sometimes work is *short-circuiting* standard procedures. An organization may not have many procedures, but people may be able to save time by short-circuiting those procedures that *do* exist. And, in a Routine organization, the voluminous procedures themselves are likely to take the blame for the overload, so short-circuiting them will occur to everyone as a source of relief.

In a long-term crisis, however, the short-circuiting tactic is used for so long that it becomes part of standard operating procedure. People routinely sign off that they have completed tasks that they haven't even started. Checkmarks go in boxes on the project schedule, which everyone knows is a fantasy anyway. Everyone, that is, except the Routine project manager.

In the early stages of a long crisis, you'll hear a lot of complaining about procedures. Later, the complaining stops, and the managers feel better. But the complaining has stopped because people have learned to avoid the procedures they can escape. By not complaining, they don't draw attention to what they're doing—or, rather, not doing.

6.3.1 The Boomerang Effect

The pressure of the exponential increase in the number of quality problems leads to a second-order type of increase. The incessant pressure tempts people at all levels of the organization to take shortcuts, hoping that quality will "somehow come out all right." It won't. The end result of the shortcuts is a "boomerang" effect—things take longer, not shorter:

Attempts to shortcut quality always make the problem worse.

Why is this boomerang inevitable? Figure 6-6 illustrates one common cycle of effects. The cycle can start anywhere, so there is no sense trying to determine which action comes "first." Perhaps increased problem demand or customer demand resulted in a product shipment that was not well accepted by the customers, so that the organization was flooded with STIs. Perhaps a manager made poor schedule estimate and then insisted on saving face by pushing the product out the door before its time. In any case, once the cycle started, it seemed to be off "on its own."

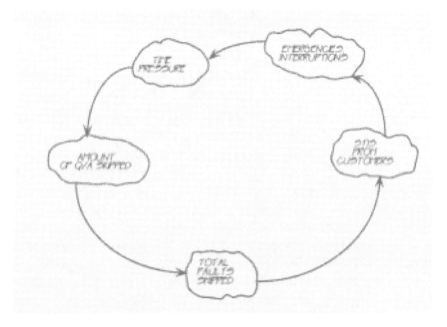

Figure 6-6. Boomerang effects of shortcuts on quality can easily become self-perpetuating.

But Figure 6-6 doesn't tell the whole awful story. The cycle of Figure 6-6 will not go away "by itself." If it is not arrested quickly by effective management action, it starts to become established as part of the culture of the organization. Soon, the development process itself begins to deteriorate in irreversible ways, as suggested in Figure 6-7. Let's look at some of the effects wrapped up in this diagram, most of which we've already studied as separate dynamics in their own right.

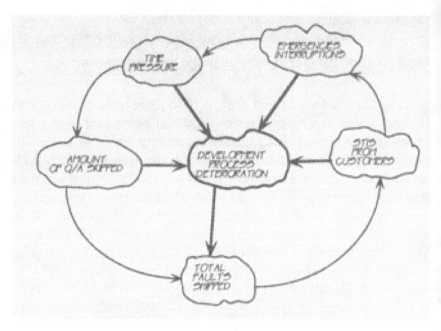

Figure 6-7. If the boomerang effects of shortcuts on quality continue for any length of time, they begin to eat away at the quality of the process itself, which in turn further increases the total faults shipped. The organization is now on a serious downward spiral.

6.3.2 The decision to ship poor quality

When the promised shipping date comes, Routine managers may be embarrassed to admit that they can neither predict outcomes nor control them. They can cope with the immediate clamor by shipping "as is." This tactic does buy them some immediate, short-term relief from the clamor, because it takes time for the pipeline to fill so that the feedback about failures to

174

complete the return cycle. Perhaps before that happens, they will be promoted for "successfully" shipping the product.

Soon, however, the pipeline fills. As a result of trying to meet schedules by shipping poor quality, the eventual schedule performance becomes worse—a perfect boomerang. If the original managers are lucky, however, the boomerang hits their successors.

6.3.3 Bypassing quality assurance

One of the ways to save time in shipping is to bypass quality assurance, or at least skimp on quality assurance effort–the effort to see that all quality-oriented steps are carried out. Not only does this save steps in the process, but the less quality assurance work you do, the fewer failures you see. The fewer failures you see, the easier it is to believe that "the quality is okay," and thus make the decision to ship the product.

In such a situation, Routine managers may confidently say, "We will ship no product before its time." But by skimping on quality assurance, they have cut off the information that would let them know if it's time to ship the product.

This self-induced illusion that there aren't so many faults results in more faults being shipped to the field. These faults come back later, in a less disciplined environment, resulting in even more faults—another perfect boomerang.

6.3.4 Emergencies and interruptions

When failures return, there is a corresponding increase in the number of interruptions and emergency situations coming from the system's users. The result is a miserable work environment, which increases time pressure and disrupts the development process for items in process. These new projects will be full of faults and behind schedule, just like previous projects. These then lead to more emergencies and interruptions, and the boomerang returns again.

6.3.5 Morale effects

Perhaps the most striking effect of shipping a product "before its time" is that the technical staff sees this decision as a betrayal by management. Management may be judged by upper management on cost and schedule, but the technical staff judge themselves on the quality of their work. And they are harsh judges, and the thought that they are shipping garbage puts them into a deep depression. In this state, they have no motivation to maintain the process, let alone to improve it (Figure 6-8).

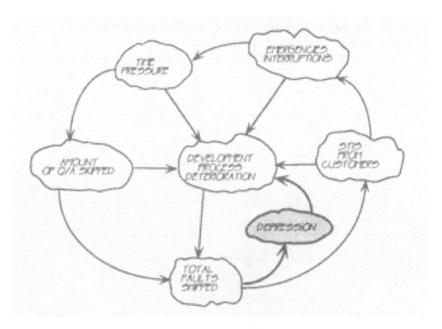

Figure 6-8. The decision to ship a product known to be of poor quality product sends the development staff into a deep depression, which has destructive effects on future process quality.

A decision to ship poor quality is interpreted in various ways by the technical staff:

1. *Managers are stupid*—they don't know enough to recognize quality.

2. *Managers are dishonest*—they know the quality is poor, and they're trying to fool the customers.

3. *Managers are spineless*—they know they can't fool the customers, but they are too afraid of their own managers to stand up for what's right.

4. *Managers are greedy*—they could stand up to their managers, but they want to get promoted and get away with personal gain.

You can take your pick of interpretations, because none of them leads to a well-motivated technical staff, and development quality immediately begins to suffer noticeably.

6.3.6 Managers are human

Technical staff always interpret management decision to ship a poor quality product as a betrayal of trust. Once this happens, they feel they can never count on their managers again. It's unfortunate that the technical staff hardly ever makes a fifth interpretation:

5. *Managers are trying to be helpful*—but managers are human, just like the technical staff.

If this kind of trust has been established *before* the organization goes into a boomerang cycle, there's a much better chance of them getting out before it degenerates into a downward spiral. Once the boomerang starts, however, managers cannot build trust by telling the staff, "Trust me!"

6.4 How Customers Impact the Boomerang

The boomerang cycle may have started because of customer demand, especially in an organization that sells software to many customers. The more people who use the system after it is released, the worse the effect. Let's see why.

6.4.1 More failure reports

The difficulty may start with yielding to customer pressure to ship a product, but as soon as the customers start using the product, they start generating STIs. The more customers there are, of course, the more STIs come in, so the more emergencies and interruptions there are to disrupt the development process.

6.4.2 Multiplying costs after release

Because each system goes out in multiple copies, shipping an error means multiplying the costs of finding that error and correcting it. Some of these costs may be hidden from the people in software development, because they are incurred in the field environment, but many of them come back as STIs and interruptions. We know the effect that interruptions and a heavy workload of fixes has on the development process. The workload increases, and the mistakes increase—two more boomerangs.

6.4.3 Increased temptation

Paradoxically, the "ship anyway" tactic seems most tempting for software products with many customers. The pressure to ship may be much greater, coming as it does from so many customers, with a large multiplier on income from the product. This pressure may be particularly strong on new "error-correcting" versions of the software, which may decrease the time of the release cycle, thus further increasing the pressure on the development organization.

On the other hand, first releases generate pressure because of the fear of "losing market share" if the product is late to market. Once the customers buy a copy, it will be easy to sell them a "fix-release." It will even generate extra income.

Individual software systems with a single customer generally don't have a series of long delays in the cycle from developer to customer to developer. They've learned that shipping faults to the customer will buy them little, if any, time, even in the short run. Also, their customer may have learned the folly of pressing for delivery of a system that doesn't work right.

6.4.4 The final solution

There is, of course, one stabilizing dynamic, but it's not very cheerful. If the releases are bad enough, the number of customers will start to decrease, thus relieving some of the pressures. Customers tell other customers, and somebody tells the press.

How strong is this effect? In a classic study of word-of-mouth effects, the Coca-Cola company analyzed complaints from consumers in 1980.

180

"Customers who complained and weren't satisfied with the response typically told 8 to 10 friends or associates about their experience, and, in 12% of the cases, told more than 20 people. And complainers did more than gripe: 30% said they stopped buying Coca-Cola products altogether and another 45% said they'd buy less in the future. If the complaint was resolved satisfactorily—as 85% were—the average consumer told 4 or 5 people about it and, in 10% of the cases, also bought more of the company's products."

If you attend user-group meetings, you can confirm that software users are at least as unforgiving as Coke drinkers. And many experiences with failed personal computer software products show that once the first flush of novelty has worn off, buyers know what's good and what's bad, and won't buy anything that has the scent of poor quality.

In other words, it may not be fair, but the arithmetic of word-of-mouth is very strongly biased against shippers of poor quality. Work out the dynamics of this biased reporting, and you'll see why poor quality hurts you much more than good quality helps. Pretty soon, the number of new customers starts to decrease, and if things get bad enough, faithful customers stop using the product.

However, once the organization actually starts losing customers, other pressures mount to more than compensate for this effect. The eventual result of shipping poor quality is loss of revenue through installation delays, poor reputation, and cancelled orders. In many organizations, the final result is lawsuits for non-performance of contracts or simply going out of business. Failure of management to control this poor quality cycle is undoubtedly the major cause of failure among software organizations today.

6.5 Helpful Hints and Suggestions

• A rule of thumb can help when estimating the effects of splitting tasks. The following table is what I use:

Number of Tasks % on Each

1.....100%

2......40%

3......20%

4......10%

5........5%

>5.....random

Sometimes you do better than this for certain people for short periods of time, but if you plan on it, your plan will fail.

• The Priority Dynamic, when tied to money, produces the Law of Supply and Demand, because more priority (higher prices) will lead to more capacity (greater supply). If you don't want prices to rise, you may want to use some artificial limited resource to regulate the priority system. In that case, however, the one who limits the resource needs to be able to resist the seduction of "just once" granting an exemption.

6.6 Summary

1. Software projects commonly break down when the reality of time finally forces them to realize where they actually are. When this happens, however, the symptoms displayed are unique to each project and each individual.

2. Many symptoms are equivalent to shuffling work around, accomplishing nothing or, even worse, actually sending the project backwards. One such backwards dynamic is the attempt to beat Brooks's Law through splitting tasks among existing workers.

3. Ineffective priority schemes are common ways of doing nothing. These including setting everything to number one priority, choosing your own priority independent of project priority, or simply doing the easiest task first.

4. A final way of doing nothing is to circulate "hot potatoes," which are tasks that management counts against you if they are on your desk when "measurement" time comes.

5. There are a number of ways to observe that managers are actually doing nothing. They may

   • be accepting poor quality products

   • not be accepting schedule slippage

   • be accepting of resource overruns

   • be unavailable to their workers

   • assert that they have no time to do the project right

6. A sure sign that a project is breaking down under time pressure is when managers and workers start short-circuiting procedures. This invariable creates a boomerang effect in which the very quality the manager intended to improve is made worse by the short-circuiting action.

7. The decision to ship poor quality to save time and resources always creates a boomerang effect. Bypassing quality assurance is similar. Both of these tactics lead, among other things, to destruction of the development process, more emergencies and interruptions, and devastation of morale.

8. When morale deteriorates into project depression, process quality will not be maintained, let alone improved. Trust built before the crisis will help an organization recover more quickly, but attempts to build trust during the crisis will probably backfire —especially if they are in the form of telling: "Trust me!"

9. Multiple customers increase the pressure on the boomerang cycle, up to the point that the resultant poor quality drives away customers, thus stabilizing the organization—or killing it.

6.7. Practice

1. Draw a diagram of effects showing how money or other rationed quantity can stabilize a priority system. Give three examples of the kinds of actions that can disrupt such as system, and show how they would affect your diagram.

2. What kinds of management activities will build a cushion of trust that can help an organization pull itself out of a boomerang cycle? What activities tend to destroy trust?

3. Work out a diagram of effects of number of customers on the boomerang effect. Include the effects of biased reporting of failures, and show why poor quality hurts you much more than good quality helps.

Chapter 7: What We've Managed To Accomplish

"Truth emerges more readily from error than from confusion." - Sir Frances Bacon

Looking back over this volume, what seems to emerge is a sad story of error and confusion in the software industry. To reach such a conclusion would be to commit a selection fallacy, for although it's a story of error and confusion, it's not a sad story at all. Although there has been no shortage of sad events, the software industry as a whole has accomplished remarkable things in the past 40 years. In order that we don't end on a fallacious note, it's time to take stock of where we've been—and where we're going—both in this book and in the software industry.

7.1. Why Systems Thinking?

One of the most frightening events of my life was to wake up one morning and find that I had been transformed from a competent programmer to an incompetent manager of programmers. The stroke of a pen was all it took to change my title, but I don't know how long it would take to make me as competent a manager as I was a programmer. It certainly didn't happen overnight.

Over the years, I've learned that being a programmer is rather poor preparation for becoming a manager of programming, for several reasons:

1. An effective manager requires excellent observation skills. Working alone as a programmer, starting at a screen all day, is poor training for observation skills.

2. An effective manager must be able to act congruently in difficult interpersonal situations. Interacting with an unemotional machine is no training at all for handling human emotions. On the other hand, programming is at least partial preparation for one aspect of the managing programming:

3. An effective controller needs models of the system being controlled. Working as a programmer supplies some raw data that can be food for dynamic models of the software process. Moreover, the thought processes in programming are logical, and train us in the kind of thinking that we need to make usable models.

Programmers with any skill at all appreciate the value of planning. Good programmers start a project with a clear idea of what they intend to do. They also have a clear idea of what isn't clear yet—what needs to be clear before they're finished. This is exactly what good managers need to do. When I woke up a manager, I would have been lost without my systems thinking abilities. Using these abilities, I was often able to work out

- what things to observe
- what meaning to make of my observations

• what actions to take to achieve my goals.

In other words, for me, the study of systems thinking comes naturally before the study of observation and action. In my struggle to become an effective manger, my thinking ability often pulled me through error and confusion, which is why I believe improved thinking will help other people trying to make the same transition.

7.2. Why Manage?

After reading some of the horror stories in this volume, why would anyone *want* to manage software? It can't be the money. If you're interested in money, you'd probably do better investing your time in becoming a top developer, rather than take a chance on becoming a mediocre manager. It can't be the admiration of your peers, because they'll probably despise you for "selling out" to management.

Over the years, I've found very few programmers who went into management for money or prestige. Instead, I've met thousands of them who went into management for the same reason so many abused children become therapists. It's called the "wounded healer" syndrome: you take up healing because of the experience with your own wounds. Programmers go into management because they have a cause: they think they can make the software business better than it is.

It was that way for me. When I was a programmer, I had such

insufferable experiences with management that I knew I would be able to do a better job. I was wrong. Like many programmers, I was exactly the wrong type of person to take up management. I was afraid of people. I didn't even like people unless they were techies like me. I couldn't look people straight in the eye when I talked to them—unless I was shouting blame at them. I hadn't the foggiest idea of how to get people to understand me, and no idea at all of how to understand them—even if I had wanted to. I had no social skills—I didn't know how to dress, to eat in public, or to carry on polite conversation. In short, I was a consummate nerd.

I *still* don't know how to dress, to eat in public, or to carry on polite conversation, but in 40 years I've learned a few of the other things—mostly the hard way, but also by some dedicated study. I think that today I can be a pretty good manager, but how many of our software managers have had 40 years to learn their trade? Like me, most of them had to learn in their sleep the night they got "promoted" from programmer to manager.

Our business is still too young and growing too fast. We haven't had the luxury of developing competent managers the way they are ripened in construction, manufacturing, finance, or any other sensible trade. We have neither the centuries of experience nor the luxury of slow apprenticeship.

What we do have is *dedication to a cause*, and that keeps us going even when we know we are managing poorly, or being

189

managed poorly. We *know* in our deepest way of knowing that computers can make a difference in the world—a difference for the good. That's why we exchange the fun and acclaim of programming for the agony and ridicule of managing—*helping others use their programming talents to make a difference in the world.*

That's why I became an ex-programmer to try my hand at managing. That's why I've spent the past 20 years or so training other ex-programmers to be better managers. That's why I've written this book, and I certainly hope that's why you're reading it.

7.3. Estimating Our Accomplishments

So, have we made a difference in the world, or have we sold our birthright for a mess of pottage? If you read the newspapers, you might believe it's all pottage, because they're full of stories of how horrible we are. But reviewing my 40 years in the software business, I'd have to say that we've made enormous progress.

7.3.1. Productivity increases

A few years ago, I made an estimate of Pattern 0 progress using my own experience:

In 1956,... I had a chance to write my first real application program. Working with a young civil engineer, Lyle Hoag, I wrote a program to analyze hydraulic networks—the systems that serve the water needs of a city. ...

(In 1979) using my IBM 5110 and programming in APL, I reproduced that application from the past in order to see if my productivity as a programmer had increased. In 1956, two of us worked more than four weeks, full-time plus lots of overtime to write and test our system. In 1979, I produced a version 2 of the program in about two and a half hours work, and increase in productivity of over 200 times. That amounts to over 25 percent per year, ...

This level of productivity increase is an astonishing accomplishment for our industry, and not at all consonant with the lamentations of the press. According to the received wisdom, programming productivity has increased less than 3% per year, though I've never seen anyone justify this oft-repeated figure. Moreover, I now hear that productivity increases are declining in recent years—but that's what I've heard every year for at least 30 years. And, curiously enough, I always hear these figures from someone who is selling a new productivity tool.

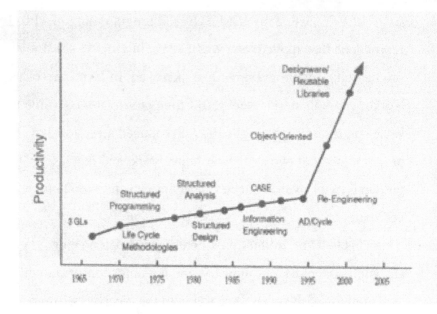

Figure 7-1. The accepted wisdom about software productivity, given at many conferences, without proof or evidence, over the the 25 years from the 1960s to the 1990s, with extrapolation from there according to the claims of a couple of the hot new topics of the time. If we would adjust the curve to the actual experience to 2010, we'd see that it's just the same old creep– albeit upwards. And if we add the 2010 fads' claims, we'd see the same sharp increase predicted. <sigh> No, we never learn. Only the labels change.

Figure 7-1 reproduces a graph I've seen several times at software engineering conferences. No source is given—the graph is presented as if everyone knows it is "the truth." Although "productivity" is never defined and the Y-axis is never scaled, the message it presents could be expressed this way:

"For the past 25-45 years, we've seen new technologies appearing approximately every 4 years. They promise fantastic increases in productivity, but you can see from the chart that productivity growth has been much slower than "fantastic." However, in the next few years, productivity is really going to take off, if you use Scrum, or XP, or Rails, or Ruby on Rails, or .... This time, unlike all the other times, the promise of the technology *will* be realized. Why? Because I say so." (Sure!)

If the perspective of 50 years in the software business is worth anything, it saves me the time wasted looking at these graphs and saying, "Gee whiz!"

Sometimes, the graph is supported by another slide that gives "real numbers" on "assimilation of new technologies." Here's a typical example:

• Only 10% of software organizations have a Life-Cycle methodology that is accepted and consistently used.

• Only 15% use structured programming.

• Only 12% do structured analysis.

• Only 15% have some form of CASE tool in use.

The repeated word "only" suggests that the anonymous author feels the usage of these tools should be greater. The message continues,

"Although most organizations never used these previous tools (which is why they didn't help productivity that much), *my* new tool will be different. *Everyone* will use it, and so productivity will shoot up into the sky like an arrow." (Applause!)

7.3.2. Why we're suckers for magic bullets

Why, over 40 years or more, have we continued to be suckers for the continuing promise of "magic bullets" that will suddenly increase productivity? Perhaps it has to do with the reasons we chose to go into this business in the first place. Each of us wants to be recognized for a great innovation that helps the world, and in the early days, everything *was* an innovation—not because we pioneers were so brilliant, but just because there were no computers available to anyone before we came along. We got an undeserved reputation for being innovative, and we got hooked by our own reputation.

We also biased the reporting. The Time article quoted in the Preface goes on to say,

Will the time come at last when the machines rule—perhaps without seeming to rule—as the mysterious "spirit of the colony" rules individual ants?

To all such chilling speculation, the young engineers in Professor Aiken's laboratory have a breezy answer: "When a machine is acting badly, we consider it a responsible person and blame it for its stupidity. When it's doing fine, we say it is a tool that we clever humans built."

Even 40 years ago we blamed the machine for the failures, while taking personal credit for the successes. Nowadays, there are more systems to fail, and fewer easy innovations. Everyone still wants to be the first to do something, but most of the "innovations" are clones, or clones with small variations, as in natural selection. When seen through its cumulative effects over decades, this kind of evolutionary progress is astounding—25% increase in individual productivity per year. But we don't consider it astounding, because it doesn't get us the applause we crave.

7.3.3. Pattern 1 productivity; Pattern 2 ambition

Another reason we don't consider this predicted 25% annual increase astounding is that it's merely Pattern 1 productivity. As our productivity grew, so did our ambition. Soon, we were attempting systems that one person could not implement, and so we tried to put together the software cultures of Pattern 2.

In this process of routinizing programming, we lost some of that 25% per year we might have had. We lost productivity for all the systems reasons given in this volume, and for others besides. For example, there has been a continuous removal of our most experienced programmers to become managers. So, our accomplishments are not living up to our ambitions, but, for many of our customers, it's still been worth it.

7.4 What Each Pattern Has Contributed

How can we keep a proper perspective on our own accomplishments? Perhaps we should stop struggling from time to time and take a quick review of what each pattern has accomplished, without any ulterior motive such as selling software tools. Let's try it now.

7.4.1. Pattern 0: Oblivious

Even a cursory review would show the accomplishments of Pattern 0. Today, literally millions of people can solve many of their own problems without the intervention of computer specialists. To a great extent, we have democratized the software business and weakened the caste system of "young engineers." I believe we can take credit for this transformation. Cheap hardware takes some of the credit, of course, but without good personal software, cheap hardware would have fallen under the control of the existing software hierarchy.

A few years ago I heard something on the radio news that marked our Pattern 0 progress better than any productivity measure. A space shuttle launch had been delayed because of "computer malfunction," and the newscaster said, "Isn't it amazing that an entire mission can be delayed by the failure of something so common and ordinary as a computer!"

The accomplishment of Pattern 0 is precisely in "making

computers ordinary"—making them something about which we can indeed be *oblivious*.

7.4.2. Pattern 1: Variable

I've already indicated my own measure of Pattern 1 accomplishments—perhaps 25% per year increase in individual programmer productivity. Pattern 1 is where most of the big innovations have come from, but we still haven't learned how to innovate on demand. You don't command someone to go out and invent something as revolutionary as a spreadsheet, yet I don't think that's a criticism of what we've done to improve Pattern 1.

Of course, Pattern 1 suffers a bit because all the programmers are trying to make revolutionary innovations. I recently read a summary of more than 200 CASE tools on the market for the IBM PC. More recently, when a new eReader was introduced, the vendor claimed it already had 200,000 applications. Did each "inventor," each "programmer," think that this was the real thing? Given the 25% increase in productivity, I suppose we can absorb a small overhead in Pattern 1 to feed the vanity expressed in that famous MIT graffito:

"I'd rather write programs that write programs than write programs."

7.4.3. Pattern 2: Routine

The accomplishments of Pattern 2 are difficult to detect,

197

because the job of Pattern 2 is making software work routine. Moreover, their positive accomplishments tend to be erased in our minds by a few spectacular failures. For these reasons, I always recommend to Pattern 2 organizations that they take an inventory of their accomplishments, to counteract their tendency to dwell on failures.

Another reason we tend to underestimate Pattern 2 accomplishments is the software industry's tendency to focus on tools rather than on people. For instance, Phil Crosby's first emphasis in any quality program is "management understanding and attitude." Isn't it curious, then, that in the original IBM articles tying the software industry to Crosby's work, the authors simply dropped all of Crosby's remarks about managers.

If you knew Crosby only through these IBM articles, you would never imagine that he considers management the number one factor in improving quality. You would get the impression that quality improvement comes primarily through "process, methodologies, adherence to process, tools, change control, data gathering, communication and use of data, goal setting, quality focus, customer focus, and technical awareness," the items in IBM's "process grid." How curious that fifty years ago, IBM's articles claimed that quality and productivity came from *business machines*.

All of these items are important to software management, but the omission of management thinking, observing, and acting is a typical Pattern 2 blind spot. To Pattern 2 managers, these items *are* management, the things they had to struggle with to become Pattern 2 managers. But they're *not* all there is to management. This omission of management is not just an IBM bias. It's typical of the software industry over the past 50 years.

And make no mistake, the major contribution of Pattern 2 is a contribution to management. Pattern 2 managers may not handle the extraordinary very well, but they have succeeded in making ordinary things ordinary. That may not seem very dramatic, but I think we wouldn't need so much drama if we were secure in our solid contributions to the world.

7.4.3. Pattern 3, 4, and 5

Up until now, Patterns 3, 4, and 5 haven't made many great contributions to the welfare of the world, because up until now, very few software cultures have arrived at Patterns 3, 4, or 5. We do have examples to show that Pattern 3, through steering, knows how to make *extraordinary things ordinary*, thus correcting some of the deficiencies of Pattern 2. Perhaps this book will make an incremental contribution to the realization of that Pattern 3 promise.

We also know enough of the promise of Pattern 4 to believe that it will help in make things more *efficient*. Though Pattern 5 remains largely a vision, we believe it will help by making good cultural practices *transferrable*, and propagating them through the generations.

7.5. Meta-patterns

All in all, we have every reason to expect that the productivity curve, regardless of how it is measured, will continue to rise for the next 50 years. For one thing, this has been the experience in other engineering disciplines. For another, we have not only done better, but signs show we're *getting better at getting better*. These signs are what I call the "meta-patterns."

Meta- patterns are patterns not just for one organization, but for the whole software industry. Meta-patterns are not just the incremental improvements from month to month or year to year, but are those accumulated small steps that are improving quality over generations.

Even though our industry is still young, we can already see what each pattern has contributed to the meta-pattern. Pattern 0 has been removing the fear of computers. Pattern 1 has been developing individual prowess. Pattern 2 has been bringing order to disorder, automating what it can, but leaving the hardest problems to be solved by effective management. Pattern 3 is bringing better management to software, eliminating disasters, which may bring us better press—though I doubt whether journalists will ever lose their ability to capitalize on the sensational.

The successes of all these patterns are allowing our aspirations to rise, creating new problems, but also new opportunities to make the world a better place. Pattern 4 promises to improve the orderliness of our business, automating many of the routines for arising from Pattern 2, and making them efficient enough for general use. And Pattern 5, we hope, will create the global environment for software progress, setting the next iteration of hope, struggle, and improvement for everyone.

It is this vision that permits us to carry on through some of our stupid failures. And carry on we must, because, as R.R. Whyte said in one of my most favorite engineering books, *Engineering Progress Through Trouble* (1975):

"One begins to recognize that falling into trouble, encountering some unexpected difficulty however harassing at the time, is in fact an opportunity for making a fresh advance and most advances in engineering have in fact been made by turning failure into success."

In other words, it's not the events that count, but your reaction to those events. You can't always be a winner, and you won't always be a loser. But you can always be a *learner*. That's why we've managed to accomplish so much, and that's why we'll continue to accomplish even more.

7.6 Helpful Hints and Suggestions

• We are not alone among the engineering disciplines, but we are the youngster. We can learn a great deal by studying the history of other engineering disciplines. Perhaps we cannot avoid their mistakes, but at least we can learn faster from our own.

• We can also learn from our own experiences, but these are not as well documented yet as the experiences of other disciplines. Still, we have each other as valuable sources of living history, which is in some ways better than a book. Take the time to share your experiences with others.

7.7 Summary

1. In spite of the impression we might get from studying our failures, we've managed to accomplish a great deal in the past 4 decades of the software industry.

2. One of the reasons we've accomplished a great deal is the quality of our thinking, which is the strongest asset many of us have, when we use it.

3. Our industry has probably suffered because of the process by which we select our managers. People who select themselves into programming work probably are not the best "naturals" for management jobs. Nevertheless, they could learn to do a good job of managing, if they were given the training. As long as we don't honor management, however, they're not likely to receive one-tenth the management training they need.

4. The accomplishments of the software industry are much greater than you would believe if you listened to the purveyors of software and hardware tools. It is in their interest to make us believe that we're not doing very well, but that their tool will be the magic bullet we need.

5. We tend to be suckers for magic bullets because we want to accomplish great things, but great things are usually accomplished through a series of small steps, contrary to the popular image.

6. We may fail to recognize how much our productivity has increased because we are so ambitious. Once we succeed in doing something well, we immediately attempt something more grand, without stopping to take stock of our accomplishments.

7. Each pattern has contributed to the development of our industry. Pattern 0 has made computers less frightening to the general public. Pattern 1 has made many innovations that have contributed to our productivity. Pattern 2 has strung these innovations together into methodologies that make it possible to complete many larger projects in routine ways. Pattern 3 has taught us what is needed to keep even larger projects under control. The contributions of Patterns 4 and 5 are still more in terms of visions of possibilities, but that's as important to progress as actual accomplishments.

8. Meta-patterns are the development patterns of the culture of the industry as a whole. Once again, each pattern has

contributed to the development of meta-patterns, and we are not only learning to handle software, but are learning how to learn to handle software.

7.8 Practice

1. If you work in a Pattern 2 organization, take an inventory of the positive accomplishments made in the past year. How many times did people get off track and start to talk about failures? What insights did you get in making this inventory?

2. If you are a programmer, make a serious estimate of how much your personal productivity has improved over the course of your career. Make a list of the things that have contributed to your improvement. What will make the next increment of improvement?

3. Why did you become a programmer? Why did you become a manager? Which of your reasons for becoming a programmer qualify you to become a manager? Which ones tend to disqualify you?

4. Recall some failure in which you played a part. What did you lose? What did you learn? On balance, was it worth it? What could you have done to increase your learning?

5. Share your failure experience with some colleagues. What can you conclude from the commonality of your experiences of failure? Of your reactions to failure? Then share a success

experience and ask the same questions. Do you learn more from failures or successes? Why?

Appendix A: The Diagram of Effects

One of the important skills of Steering managers is the ability to reason about non-linear systems. One of the favorite tools for thinking about non-linear systems is the *diagram of effects* . Figure A-1 is an example of a diagram of effects showing some effects of management pressure to resolve software failures (STIs). We can use this diagram to explain the major notational conventions of the diagram of effects.

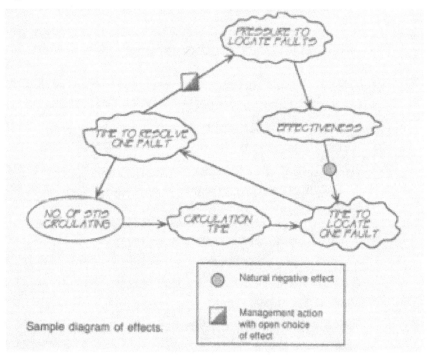

Figure A-1. A diagram of effects.

A diagram of effects consists primarily of nodes connected by arrows:

1. Each node stands for a measurable quantity, like circulation time, effectiveness, time to locate one fault, or pressure to locate faults. I use the "cloud" symbol rather than a circle or rectangle to remind us that nodes indicate *measurements*, not *things or processes* as in flow charts, data flow diagrams, and the like.

2. These cloud nodes may represent actual measurements, or they may represent conceptual measurements—things that could be measured, but are not measured at present. They may be too expensive to measure, or not worth the trouble, or just not happen to be measured yet. The important thing is that they *could* be measured—perhaps only approximately—if we were willing to pay the price.

3. When we wish to indicate an actual measurement currently being made, we use a very regular, elliptical "cloud," as we see for "number of STIs circulating." Most of the time, however, we'll use effects diagrams for *conceptual*—rather than mathematical— analysis, so most of the clouds will be appropriately rough.

4. An arrow from node A to node B indicates that quantity A has an *effect* on quantity B. We may actually know the effect in one of three ways:

a. We have a mathematical formula for the effect, as in

time to locate one fault = circulation time + other factors

b. The effect is deduced from observations. For instance,

207

we've seen people get nervous and lose their effectiveness when under pressure from management.

c. The effect may be inferred from past experience. For instance, we've noticed on other projects how management changes the pressure when fault resolution time changes.

5. The general direction of the effect of A on B may be indicated by the presence or absence of the gray dot on the arrow between them.

a. No dot means that as A moves in one direction, B moves in the *same* direction. (*More* STIs circulating means *more* circulation time; *less* STIs circulating means *less* circulation time.)

b. A dot on the arrow means that as A moves in one direction, B moves in the *opposite* direction. (*More* effectiveness means *less* time to locate one fault; *less* effectiveness means *more* time to locate one fault.)

6. Squares on an effects line indicate that human intervention is determining the direction of the effect:

a. A white square means the human intervention is making the affected measurement move in the same direction to the movement of the cause (just as a plain arrow indicates a *natural* same direction).

b. A gray square means the human intervention is making the affected measurement move in the opposite direction to the movement of the cause (just as a gray dot indicates a *natural* opposite direction).

a. A white/gray square means the human intervention can make the affected measurement move in the same or the opposite direction to the movement of the cause, depending on the intervention. In this case, management can react to increased fault resolution time by either increasing or decreasing pressure to locate faults.

Appendix B: The Software Engineering Cultural Patterns

In these volumes, we've made extensive use of the idea of software cultural patterns. For ease of reference, this appendix will summarize various aspects of those cultural patterns.

To my knowledge, Crosby was the first to apply the idea of cultural patterns to the study of industrial processes. Crosby discovered that the various processes that make up a technology don't merely occur in random combinations, but in coherent patterns.

In their article, "A Programming Process Study," Radice, et al. adapted Crosby's "stratification by quality" scheme to software development. In his book, *Managing the Software Process* , Watts Humphrey of the Software Engineering Institute (SEI) extended their work and identified five levels of "process maturity" through which a software development organization might grow.

Other software engineering observers quickly noted the usefulness of Humphrey's maturity levels. Bill Curtis, then of MCC, and now at SEI, proposed a "software human resource maturity model" with five levels.

I believe that each of these models represents points of view of the same phenomenon. Crosby named his five patterns based largely on the *management attitudes* to be found in each. The names used by SEI are more related to the *types of processes* found in each pattern, rather than to the attitudes of management, a la Crosby. Curtis made his classification on the basis of *the way people were treated* within the organization.

In my own work with software engineering organizations, I most often use the cultural view combined with Crosby's original focus on management, and on attitudes, but find each view useful at various times. The following summary incorporates material from each point of view.

Pattern 0. Oblivious Process

Other Names: Doesn't exist in Crosby, Humphrey, or Curtis models.

Metaphor: Walking: When you want to go somewhere, you just go.

View of themselves: "We don't even know that we're performing a process."

Management understanding and attitude: No comprehension that quality is a management issue.

Problem handling: Problems are suffered in silence.

Summation of quality position: "We don't have quality problems."

When this pattern is successful: To succeed, the individuals
need three conditions:

  a. I'm solving my own problems.
  b. Those problems aren't too big for what I know is
technically possible.
  c. I know what I want better than anyone else.
  Process results. Results depend totally on the individual. No
records are kept, so we don't have measurements. Because the
customer is the developer, delivery is always acceptable.

Pattern 1: Variable Process

  Other Names:

    Crosby: ======Uncertainty Stage
    Humphrey: ======Initial Process
    Curtis:============Herded
  View of themselves: "We do whatever we feel like at the
moment."

  Metaphor: Riding A Horse: When you want to go
somewhere, you saddle up and ride ... if the horse cooperates.

  Management understanding and attitude: No
comprehension of quality as a management tool.

  Problem handling: Problems are fought with inadequate
definition and no resolution—plus lots of yelling and accusations.

  Summation of quality position: "We don't know why we
have quality problems."

When this pattern is successful: To succeed, the individuals (or teams) need three conditions:

> a. I have great rapport with my customer.
> b. I'm a competent professional individual.
> c. Customer's problem isn't too big for me.

Process results: The work is generally one-on-one, customer and developer. Quality is measured internally by "it works," externally by relationship quality. Emotion, personal relations, and mysticism drive everything. There is no consistent design, randomly structured code, errors removed by haphazard testing. Some of the work is excellent, some is bizarre—all depending on the individual.

Pattern 2: Routine Process

Other Names:

> Crosby: Awakening Stage
> Humphrey: Repeatable Process
> Curtis: Managed

View of themselves: "We follow our routines (except when we lose our nerve)."

Metaphor: A train: Large capacity and very efficient ... if you go where tracks are. Helpless when off the tracks.

Management understanding and attitude: Recognize that quality management may be of value, but unwilling to provide money or time to make it all happen.

Problem handling: Teams are set up to handle major problems. Long range solutions are not solicited.

Summation of quality position: "Is it absolutely necessary to have problems with quality?"

When this pattern is successful: To succeed, these organizations need four conditions:

> a. The problem is bigger than one small team can handle.
> b. The problem is not too big for our routine process.
> c. The developers conform to our routine process.
> d. We don't run into anything too exceptional.

Process results: The Routine organization has procedures to coordinate efforts—which it follows, though often in name only. Statistics on past performance are used not change, but to prove that they are doing everything in the only reasonable way. Quality is measured internally by numbers of "bugs." You generally find bottom up design, semi-structured code, with errors removed by testing and fixing. They have many successes, but a few very large failures.

Pattern 3: Steering Process

Other Names:

> Crosby: Enlightenment Stage
> Humphrey: Defined Process
> Curtis: Tailored

214

View of themselves: "We choose among our routines based on the results they produce."

Metaphor: A van: A large choice of destinations, but must generally stay on mapped roads, and must be steered to stay on road.

Management understanding and attitude: Through our quality program, we learn more about quality management, and become more supportive and helpful.

Problem handling: Problems are faced openly and resolved in an orderly way.

Summation of quality position: "Through commitment and quality improvement, we are identifying and resolving our problems."

When this pattern is successful: To succeed, these organizations need four conditions:

     a. The problem is big enough that a simple routine won't work.

     b. Our managers can negotiate with the external environment.

     c. We don't accept arbitrary schedules and constraints.

     d. We are challenged, but not excessively.

Process results: They have procedures, always well understood, but not always well-defined in writing, and which are followed even in crisis. Quality is measured by user response, but not systematically. Some measuring is done, but everybody debates which measurements are meaningful. You typically find top down design, structured code, design and code inspections, and incremental releases. The organization has consistent success, when it commits to undertake something.

Pattern 4: Anticipating Process

Other Names:

Crosby: Wisdom Stage
Humphrey: Managed Process
Curtis: Institutionalized

View of themselves: "We establish routines based on our past experience with them."

Metaphor: An airplane: Fast, reliable, and can go anywhere there's a field,... but requires large initial investment

Management understanding and attitude: Understand absolutes of quality management. Recognize their personal role in continuing emphasis.

Problem handling: Problems are identified early in their development. All functions are open to suggestion and improvement.

Summation of quality position: "Defect prevention is a routine part of our operation."

When this pattern is successful: To succeed, these organizations meet three conditions:

a. They have procedures, which they follow, and improve.

b. Quality&cost measured (internally) by meaningful statistics.

c. An explicit process group aids the process.

Process results: We may find function-theoretic design, mathematical verification, and reliability measurement. They have consistent success on ambitious projects.

Pattern 5: Congruent Process

Other Names:

Crosby: Certainty Stage
Humphrey: Optimizing Process
Curtis: Optimized

View of themselves: "Everyone is involved in improving everything all the time."

Metaphor: The Starship Enterprise: Can go where no one has gone before, can carry anything, and beam it anywhere, ... but is science fiction.

Management understanding and attitude: Consider quality management an essential part of the company system.

Problem handling: Except in the most unusual cases, problems are prevented.

Summation of quality position: "We know why we do not have quality problems."

When this pattern is successful: To succeed, these organizations meet three conditions:

      a. They have procedures which it improves, continuously.
      b. All key process variables are identified and measured automatically.
      c. Customer satisfaction drives everything.

Process results: All of the good things achievable by the other patterns, plus willingness to spend to reach next level of quality. Quality is measured by customer satisfaction and mean time to customer failure (10-100 years). Customers love the quality, and may bet their life on it. In some sense, Pattern 5 is like Pattern 0, totally responsive to the customer ... but is much better at what it does.

WHAT TO READ NEXT?

You have been reading Volume 2 of the Quality Software Series. If you found this volume useful, you may wish to continue with the other volumes of this series. You may find the entire series published a number of places, including the Kindle Store:

http://www.amazon.com/-/e/B000AP8TZ8

Below are book titles and links to web pages where you can sample Jerry's books at no cost and, if you'd like, buy them at low eBook prices in formats for all e-reading devices, or your computer.

BOOKS FOR CONSULTANTS (AND OTHERS)

The Secrets of Consulting: A Guide to Giving and Getting Advice Successfully

More Secrets of Consulting: The Consultant's Tool Kit

Are Your Lights On?: How to Know What the Problem Really Is

Weinberg on Writing: The Fieldstone Method

Experiential Learning (3 volumes)

Agile Impressions

THE QUALITY SOFTWARE SERIES

How Software is Built (Quality Software, Volume 1)

THE SYSTEMS THINKING SERIES

TECHNOLOGY/PSYCHOLOGY

The Psychology of Computer Programming

Exploring Requirements 1: Quality Before Design

Exploring Requirements 2: First Steps into Design

Perfect Software And Other Illusions About Testing

Becoming a Technical Leader

Roundtable on Technical Leadership

Roundtable on Project Management

Understanding the Professional Programmer

NOVELS: TECHNOLOGY LESSONS FRAMED IN FICTION ABOUT WOMEN OF POWER.

Freshman Murders:

> Can naive mathematicians foil a sophisticated master criminal?

Where There's a Will, There's a Murder

> How far will people go to inherit billions, free and clear?

The Death Lottery

> How can mathematicians solve serial killings based on random numbers?

First Stringers

> Six special young people become a team to defeat an armed secessionist militia.

Second Stringers

First Stringers cope with a dangerous Stringer from South America.

The Hands of God

Will a young woman's talent win her the freedom she lost when she lost both hands?

The Aremac Project

Two young inventors confront the problems accompanying fame.

Aremac Power

Successful inventors assist in protecting an abused Navajo inventor.

Mistress of Molecules

Two people from different cultures, each with incredible powers, team up.

Earth's Endless Effort

Earth's smartest living entity befriends humans to save itself from other humans.

SHORT FICTION: FUN LITTLE LESSONS.

Nine Science Fiction Stories

What can we learn from the future?

<u>Feebles for the Fable-Minded</u>:

Memorable little lessons a la Aesop.

<u>Fabulous Feebles</u>:

More Aesop-like lessons

~~~~~~